SUPER TRACTORS

SUPER
TRACTORS
Farmyard monsters from around the world

PETER HENSHAW

First published in October 2006

A catalogue record for this book is
available from the British Library

ISBN 1 84425 327 9

Library of Congress catalog card no. 2006924139

Published by Haynes Publishing,
Sparkford, Yeovil, Somerset BA22 7JJ, UK

Tel: 01963 442030 Fax: 01963 440001
Int. tel: +44 1963 442030 Int. fax: +44 1963 440001
E-mail: sales@haynes.co.uk
Website: www.haynes.co.uk

Haynes North America, Inc.,
861 Lawrence Drive, Newbury Park,
California 91320, USA

Page layout by G&M Designs Limited,
Raunds, Northamptonshire

Printed and bound in Great Britain by
J. H. Haynes & Co. Ltd, Sparkford

Contents

Foreword

by Peter Love, editor, Tractor & Machinery

Peter Love, pictured in August 2005, with a 1978 Allis-Chalmers 7580. Its days as a working tractor were coming to a close. The very complete tractor was being offered by Boothill Antiques, near Mount Pleasant, Iowa, USA. Sadly, if it didn't find a new owner soon, it was due to be scrapped.

It was a pleasure to be asked by Peter Henshaw to write a small foreword to his new book, *Supertractors*. Reading it and looking at the pictures brings back many happy memories of the places I've been to in the past 14 years, all over the world, when I took a number of the pictures featured here.

Supertractors is an interesting title: what does it mean? Well for me it is the big, powerful and impressive tractors that are, in some cases, still roaming our planet earth. That doesn't mean they were ultimately the most successful, and in some cases only a few were made. But, when produced, they were often the height of technology.

However things are changing. The huge prairie monsters, sometimes called dinosaurs, that were operated in the north of the United States, Western Canada and parts of Australia, are fast disappearing as smaller tractors are proving to be more reliable and more economic on farms with such vast acreages. In fact you sometimes see these giants spending their last days working for plant and construction companies, as experienced by myself in June 2006 during a visit to Ohio, USA.

Supertractors is a book to savour. Packed full of interesting information and glorious photography, it is a record of the passing of an era that will not be repeated.

Introduction

There are supercars, superbikes … and supertractors. A Ferrari Testarossa or a Suzuki Hayabusa are good examples of the first two, offering previously unheard of power and stratospheric top speeds. Supertractors are all about power and speed too, but not in the same way. Power certainly counts, with big turbo-intercooled diesels producing 500hp or more, but it's not sheer miles per hour that count on the farm. Instead, what makes these Ferraris of the fields into performance machines is their work rate, and here, supertractors are just as impressive as any Italian supercar.

When farms were worked by horses, an experienced ploughman with a team of two or three beasts could expect to plough an acre a day, maybe an acre and a half, given easy soil and good weather. Then came the first tractors, and even those crude early machines could plough around 10 acres a day. A modern 100hp tractor's output is much higher, able to work two acres or more an hour, but supertractor work rates can be stratospheric by comparison, ploughing an acre of land in a little more than a minute. Confront that 19th century ploughman with a modern 500hp tractor, and to him it would seem like something from outer space. But this astonishing

The Advance-Rumely Oil Pull of the 1910s, proving that big, heavy powerful tractors are not new.

Hart-Parr built tractors of up to 100hp and 26 tons.

The Fowler Gyrotiller was another massive early tractor, and a pioneer of crawler tracks.

The gargantuan six-cylinder Twin City 60-90 had a 36.5-litre engine and an all-up weight of around 14 tons.

Four-wheel drive isn't new either, with some machines pre-dating the 1920s. This is an American 4-Pull.

The Massey Harris General Purpose was a four-wheel-drive pioneer in the 1930s.

In the 1950s and '60s, specialists such as County converted two-wheel-drive Fordsons to four-wheel drive.

Roadless did a similar job to County, again converting Fordson tractors.

Four-wheel-drive conversions added no power, but plenty of traction.

performance alone does not explain why supertractors have been so successful.

In the early part of the 21st century, half the world is having second thoughts about the concept of 'big is beautiful'. Oil production has passed its peak, and global warming is accepted as a scientific reality, yet the economic bottom line of farming dictates that here at least, size matters, or at least, makes economic sense. Big supertractors can work the land so much faster than conventional machines that their extra cost is more than paid for – a 20 per cent increase in power can mean a 25 per cent increase in work rate. The extra purchase price and running costs can be recouped in two years or less.

Of course, there are downsides. As ever in the history of farming, the bigger, more expensive machines are bad news for small farms. In the late 1960s to give just one example, in California mechanical tomato pickers cut the cost of harvesting, but only the largest farms could afford them which resulted in more than 3,000 tomato growers having to sell up.

If you can afford to buy one, and keep it working, then a big tractor means bigger profits –

how different from the days of Henry Ford's original Fordson F, a mass-produced tractor so cheap that even the smallest farmer could buy one.

Supertractors by definition

What is a supertractor? There are several elements, but the essentials are four-wheel drive through equal-sized wheels, a pivot-steering (articulated) chassis, and a beefy diesel engine

These are flotation tanks, and the County Sea Horse really did float, successfully crossing the English Channel.

Steam engine builder Fowler later diversified into crawler-tracked tractors.

Smapper crawlers, such as this McCormick-Deering tractor, were used by farmers in the 1930s.

The ultimate supertractor? A little Ferguson 35 fitted with a Jaguar V12 power unit.

Supertractors, whether wheeled or tracked, and with rigid or articulated chassis, are a product of modern farming, yet most of the elements were available from the very early days of tractor technology. Take horsepower – many of the early tractors were big, heavy machines and came on the scene before the lightweights, the reason being that they were seen as natural successors to steam traction engines.

This was especially true in the USA, where farms were bigger, and the Mid West wheat prairies stretched to the far horizon. Charles Hart and Charles Parr (appropriately enough, of Charles City, Iowa), built their first production tractor in 1903. It weighed over six tons and was powered by a massive twin-cylinder engine of more than 30 litres, whose flywheel alone weighed half a ton. That first Hart-Parr tractor offered 30hp at the belt, but far bigger machines were to follow. The 60hp 'Old Reliable' was sold up to 1918, and Hart-Parr's biggest ever was the 100hp 60–100, complete with 9ft diameter driving wheels and an all-up weight of 26 tons.

producing at least 300hp. But even these aren't compulsory and few would argue that the rubber-tracked Case STX500 is not a supertractor. A JCB Fastrac does not have pivot-steering, but its pioneering role as a high-speed road tractor surely makes it qualify. The same is true of the MB-Trac, one of the first large systems tractors, with the ability to run implements both front and rear simultaneously.

The Advance-Rumely Oil Pull was similarly huge, bearing more resemblance to a traction engine than any tractor (though Hart-Parr

claimed to have coined the term 'tractor'). Powered by an oil-cooled 30-litre twin-cylinder engine, it wasn't exactly nimble, but would run all day, a source of smooth, reliable, low-revving power that was perfect for threshing work. Advance-Rumely once hitched three of these tractors to a specially made 50-furrow plough – the sort of implement a modern supertractor might use – and worked 2,000 acres in six days. The Oil Pulls were the longest lived of these early monster tractors, being built right into the 1920s. But by then, they were being outmoded by a new breed of smaller, lighter weight petrol-powered tractors that could muster 20–30hp which were relatively affordable for mid-sized farms, and far easier to use than a giant machine. In the 1930s, the most powerful row crop tractors were rated at 40hp, while the all-conquering Farmall was a 20hp machine.

The Fowler Gyrotiller was a massive rotary cultivator using a 125hp Ricardo petrol engine. Originally designed to power a military tank, the Ricardo guzzled 64 gallons of fuel per hour at full throttle. Perhaps more significant was that the Gyrotiller was a half-track design. In short, there were big, high-horsepower tractors working the

Connecting two tractors in tandem created a four-wheel drive of double the power. This was a handy solution until the mainstream factories offered their own four-wheel-drive machines.

As power outputs increased, it became difficult for two-wheel drive to cope; fitting twin rear wheels, as on this WFE, was a partial solution.

poor turning circle. It would be over 30 years before four-wheel drive entered the mainstream, although in the 1950s, British companies such as Bray, County and Roadless offered four-wheel-drive conversions of conventional Nuffield, Ford and Fordson tractors.

Crawler tracks featured early in tractor history too, and by 1908 Benjamin Holt was building large petrol-powered 'Caterpillar' tractors. The idea of a continuous crawler track was not new even then, but it worked well, and Holt's Caterpillars saw both military and farm use in the early 20th century. Holt's company merged with arch-rival Leo Best in 1925, to form the Caterpillar Tractor Company. From then on, Caterpillar would be a world leader in tracked vehicles, some of which were sold to farmers, but it would be many years before the company made its farm tractor breakthrough.

One advantage of tracks over wheels (apart from superior traction) is the ability for such a

JCB's Fastrac is the high-speed tractor of modern times, but Minneapolis-Moline in the 1930s, and this Trantor in the '70s, were there first.

Wagner pioneered the concept of a four-wheel-drive supertractor with equal-sized wheels and pivot-steer chassis.

fields long before the supertractors appeared.

Four-wheel drive isn't new either. This was actually available back in the pioneer days, even on steam traction engines, and the Four-Wheel Pull tractor, built by Olmstead of Montana, USA, was offered from 1912. Massey Harris made a more successful four-wheel drive tractor, launching the General Purpose in 1930. It had modest power (22hp at the belt), but the four equal-sized driven wheels gave it unrivalled traction and it found a niche in forestry work. However, the GP was also expensive and had a

vehicle to turn almost in its own length, and poor manoeuvrability was something that affected the Massey Harris GP in particular. Having four equal-sized wheels on a rigid chassis did not allow much clearance for the front pair to turn, and the GP was far less nimble than a little two-wheel-drive Fordson or Farmall. The answer, as adopted by all modern supertractors, is a pivot-steer, or articulated chassis, that splits in the middle to allow the rear wheels to directly follow the front. As well as giving a much tighter turning circle, this inflicts less crop damage. But here again, this is not a new idea as in 1923, Lanz built a four-wheel-drive pivot-steer version of its famous Bulldog, and a few years later the Italian Pavesi company did the same with its P4. Sales of both were disappointing, but the idea was there.

So, although supertractors in the modern sense did not appear until the late 1950s, the essential elements of their design – size, power, four-wheel drive and pivot-steering – had all been tried

before, although never brought together in one machine.

Meanwhile, what of the conventional tractors? In the 1930s, high-horsepower was restricted to crawlers from Cletrac and Caterpillar, and innovations centred on smaller tractors like the Allis-Chalmers B, or technical advances that made lightweight tractors more efficient –

Steiger was the best known of the specialist supertractor manufacturers.

If Steiger was the most recognisable supertractor, then Versatile of Canada came a very close second.

pneumatic tyres and Harry Ferguson's wonderful three-point hitch. The Second World War arrested any further developments, but as the 1950s began, there were signs that things were moving forward once again. Although diesel power was becoming dominant, manufacturers were experimenting with alternative fuels – Ford built a gas turbine tractor in the '50s, and Allis-Chalmers powered one by fuel cells. This was also the age of the multi-ratio transmission. As well as a conventional three, four, or perhaps five-speed gearbox, a two-speed range was added – Massey Ferguson's was named 'Multi-Power' – which doubled the number of ratios on offer.

One of the reasons for these transmission advances was to take advantage of increasing power. Back in the 1930s, the most powerful farm tractors produced around 40hp. In 1949, John Deere launched its biggest tractor yet, the Model R, whose 51hp could pull a five-furrow plough. In an increasingly competitive market, Deere's rivals had no choice but to respond, and the target was soon 60hp. By 1955, Oliver was selling the Super 99, all supercharged 70hp of it.

Year on year, the tractor power race went on, led by American manufacturers. In Britain and Europe, the focus was quite different, on small utility tractors like those built by Ferguson, Fiat and Ford. In the USA and Canada however, the demand for ever more power seemed insatiable. That 70hp Oliver was soon topped by the 75hp

Minneapolis-Moline Gvi (also sold with Massey-Ferguson badges, as the 97). Allis-Chalmers announced the first 100hp row-crop tractor in 1963. Powered by a new direct injection diesel of 6.9 litres, the D21 was so big that it needed a new range of implements to match, including a seven-furrow plough. A-C was first with a turbocharged tractor as well, and within a few years most of its rivals joined this new 100hp club. Like the International 1206 – prototypes of this tractor were so powerful that rear tyres buckled their sidewalls or span off the rim, so special tyres had to be made. By the end of the '60s 130hp was the new target, and it seemed as if the tractor power race would go on for ever.

Opposite: Another high-horsepower monster – Versatile's 'Big Roy', but this too never went beyond the working-prototype stage.

Above: Not all supertractors are US or Canadian built; the Belarus hailed from the USSR.

Below: Built in South Africa, the Bell was one of many low-production supertractors rarely seen outside its home country.

powered two-wheel-drive tractors, in tricky conditions, were wasting all three.

Several solutions came through in the 1960s in an attempt to make traction keep up with power, which was forging ever upwards. One was the tandem tractor, which makes an interesting diversion to the whole supertractor story. The idea was simple, to link two tractors together, the driver controlling the whole set-up from the rear machine, whose front wheels were removed. Tandem conversion kits were built in the USA, Australia and France, but perhaps the most famous was the Doe Triple-D in England. Tractor dealer Ernest Doe joined two Fordson Majors together, producing a machine with 100hp and four-wheel drive, something no other British tractor offered at the time. The Doe was later updated into a 150hp tandem based on the Ford 5000, and was built until 1966, although it was never a mainstream, mass-produced machine.

A more simple solution was to fit dual or even triple rear wheels to a conventional tractor, and many of the high horsepower two-wheel drives offered this option in the late 1960s/early '70s. The mainstream manufacturers also began to list a four-wheel drive option at the time, although in the form of 'front-wheel-assist', which was a driven front axle with small wheels. This too was

Dutra was another big four-wheel drive from behind the Iron Curtain.

Caterpillar's breakthrough with rubber tracks encouraged others to follow suit, such as this Track Marshall.

However, there was a problem. In fact, there were two – traction, and the power ambitions of some farmers. To take traction first, as power outputs grew, it became more and more difficult to transmit all that energy to the ground. Multi-speed transmissions could help, but there was only so much power that two rear tyres, however chunky, could push through wet, sticky soil. Some wheel slip is inevitable in the field, but too much slip wastes power, fuel and time – high-

a great aid to traction, but to really maximise the benefits of four-wheel drive, four equal-sized wheels were the only answer.

This was all very well, but tandems and other traction fixes just did not meet the needs of some farmers, especially in the USA. American tractor manufacturers had indulged in a power race through the 1950s and '60s, which by the middle of the second decade, resulted in some 100hp 'hotrods', whose sheer power put the inadequacy of two-wheel drive into sharp relief. Even as the mainstream factories were engaged in this power race however, the real solution to the dilemma of a high-horsepower tractor with good traction was already working on farms across Mid West America – the supertractor.

Supertractor pioneers

Elmer Wagner came up with the concept of a four-wheel-drive articulated machine as early as 1949, although it was another five years before this was applied to a farm tractor. The first Wagner tractor went on sale in 1955, as the 64hp TR-6, soon followed by the 85hp TR-9 and 160hp TR-14, all of them powered by proprietary engines. This was the first time four-wheel drive with pivot-steering had been applied to a tractor, and the Wagner was a success, more manoeuvrable than the equivalent Caterpillar crawler, and much faster.

As we have seen, there had been four-wheel-drive tractors before, but it was the pivot-steering that made it practical in the Wagner, and which

enabled the use of greater power without traction problems. The basic idea of pivot-steering, or articulation, is quite simple, and can be less complex than attempting to transmit high horsepower through a steerable front axle. Split in the middle, the tractor has two fixed axles, and pivots on two rams that give a turning angle of around 40 degrees, left or right. This makes the pivot-steer tractor surprisingly manoeuvrable for its size, and as the rear wheels follow in the tracks

The Fendt Xylon was a modern systems tractor, highly adaptable and able to perform multiple tasks.

Mercedes MB Trac 1300, another systems tractor able to carry implements front and rear simultaneously.

of the front pair, crop damage is minimised. Another advantage of pivot-steer is that both axles can oscillate independently, up to about 15° in each direction. So within those limits, all four wheels should stay in contact with the ground all the time, for maximum traction.

Pivot-steering allows the use of four big, equal-sized wheels, which bring their own benefits. Being bigger, they naturally reduce pressure on the ground over a smaller-wheeled machine – a supertractor on dual or triple wheels exerts as little as 5psi on the soil, compared with around 17psi for a conventional tractor, thus reducing soil compaction. Bigger tyres also provide more traction, so doing away with small front wheels maximises the benefits of four-wheel drive.

Top: Russian supertractors used to lag behind in technology, but as this 200hp Karkhov demonstrates, they appear to be catching up fast.

Opposite: American giant John Deere has built a long, unbroken line of supertractors from 1970 to the present day.

Above: The Claas Xerion, a modern systems tractor with four-wheel steering.

Above: Many modern supertractors are more compact than the old monsters, but are still highly efficient.

Opposite: Intensive testing is a crucial part of any supertractor's development.

Below: Not so well known outside mainland Europe, but the Doppstadt Trac is a compact, powerful machine.

As word about the Wagner tractor began to spread, so more farmers cottoned on to the benefits of running a supertractor. Sure, they were far heavier and more expensive than a conventional machine, but quicker working meant farmers were less at the mercy of the weather, and soil compaction was also reduced by fewer passes. Farmers found that a big four-wheel-drive tractor could do the work of two or even three smaller, two-wheel drives.

Two years after the Wagner was launched, Douglas and Maurice Steiger built a 130hp tractor to work their own 4,000 acre farm in Minnesota. This too had four-wheel drive and pivot-steering, and when neighbours heard what

results were being achieved, they asked the Steigers to build them one just the same. So successful was this sideline, that the Steigers became full-time tractor manufacturers, moving from the farm to a new factory in North Dakota. In 1976, their sales broached $100 million.

Wagner and Steiger were joined by a Canadian supertractor in 1966. Versatile was an established implement maker, and launched the 125hp D-100 (using a Ford diesel unit) that year. There was even a petrol version, the G-100, but Versatile's significance is that it was the first mass producer of supertractors, offering them at a lower price than Wagner or the Steigers. Versatile went on to justify its name with the first modern bi-directional tractor in 1977, although big supertractors remained a solid part of the range.

Versatile also built the world's largest tractor in 1976, the eight-wheel, eight-wheel-drive 600hp Big Roy. This certainly was big, but even this wasn't the most powerful tractor ever built. That achievement belongs to Big Bud, the last of the four big names among the supertractor specialists.

Willie Hensler was a Wagner dealer before launching Big Bud in 1969. From the start, it was clear that he had ambitions to build the largest tractors of all, and the original Big Bud was powered by a 250hp Cummins diesel, soon joined by a 350hp version, then a 450hp. The ultimate Big Bud (in terms of size) was the 16V 747. Powered by a V16 Detroit Diesel, this was

The heart of any supertractor: a straightforward, six-cylinder diesel engine of huge torque and strength …or perhaps a V8 such as this Caterpillar unit doing service in an Ag Chem Terra-Gator.

Big is beautiful? It certainly was in the late 1960s, when this Versatile left the factory.

rated at 760hp, but could be turned up to 1,000hp if required. The tyres (nearly 8ft in diameter) had to be custom-built, and the Twin Disc transmission had originally been designed for heavyweight construction machinery. At 58 tons, ready to work, the 747 was a true monster

tractor. Not for nothing did the official brochure describe it as 'Field Artillery'.

Only one 747 was ever made, and although it worked well, it never went into production – the same fate befell Big Roy. The fact was that the supertractor specialists appeared to have peaked,

and by the mid-'70s the boom years were clearly
on the way out. The reasons weren't hard to find.
The mainstream manufacturers had realised that
this was a growing sector of the market, and
decided to grab a slice for themselves. John
Deere, International, Case, Massey Ferguson and
others all launched their own big machines in the
1960s and early '70s. Most were built in the
USA, reflecting the fact that at the time, North
America remained the overwhelmingly dominant
market for such machines. Interestingly though,
the MF 1200 was built in Britain, the only true
supertractor to be so.

With greater economies of scale and some
suitable components available off the shelf, these
mainstream supertractors were often cheaper than
those of the specialists, and with a wider spread
of dealers to support them. So perhaps it was
inevitable that they would spell the beginning of
the end for pioneers like Wagner and Steiger.

As if that wasn't enough, farming took a
downturn from the late 1970s onwards, in both
Europe and North America, so even without
competition, life for specialist makers of costly
tractors was getting more difficult. Case-IH
bought up Steiger, and dropped the name (only to

*The Terra-Gator was
designed for heavy haulage
in the field; a super-truck
to complement your
supertractor?*

*Ag Chem later became
part of the AGCO empire
– another independent
specialist swallowed up.*

Tour the rural Mid West USA, and you're liable to come across plenty of moribund tractors like this one, either cannibalised for spares or just gently rotting away with the passing years.

It may be burnt out, but this John Deere could be rebuilt, or yield some reuseable parts.

1980s however, two new developments showed that there were alternatives, although rather than supplanting the conventional supertractors, they complemented them.

The first was rubber tracks. Steel-tracked crawlers were popular with some farmers right into the 1950s, especially on heavy soils where traction was a real problem. For minimising slip in glutinous conditions, they were still the best.

For all-round use though, steel tracks had many disadvantages. On tarmac roads, they were noisy, uncomfortable and extremely slow, with such vehicles managing little more than a fast walking pace while wheeled tractors could scoot along at 20mph or so. The tracks also needed a lot of maintenance, and tracked tractors were more expensive to buy in the first place. As four-wheel drive became more affordable, steel tracks rapidly fell from favour with farmers. Caterpillar tried to address the issues in 1976, with sealed and lubricated steel tracks, but on the road, these were as slow and noisy as ever.

The breakthrough came ten years later, when Caterpillar announced the Challenger, with steel-reinforced rubber tracks. Here, for the first time, was a tracked tractor that retained the huge traction benefits of tracks on heavy soil, yet could run up to 20mph on sealed roads in reasonable comfort. This was a milestone in supertractor design, and so successful was the Challenger that mainstream tractor manufacturers including John Deere and Case-IH soon unveiled their own rubber-tracked machines. This didn't spell the end for wheeled supertractors though, as both systems had their pros and cons and the wheels versus tracks debate would carry on into the 21st century.

One advantage claimed for tracks is their greater manoeuvrability than big wheels, but wheeled tractors fought back in the 1980s with four-wheel steering. This has a power limit, and lacks the ultimate tight turning of a tracked or articulated tractor, but can greatly enhance the handiness of a rigid four-wheeler. The Claas Xerion bi-directional tractor can angle all four wheels the same way, to allow the tractor to move sideways, crab-like, across the field. JCB's Quadtronic system actually offers five different modes, including 'proportional tracking', which steers the rear wheels one degree for every two degrees at the front.

bring it back, in response to the cries of outrage); Versatile was eventually swallowed by New Holland, and Big Bud concentrated on servicing and rebuilding its existing machines instead of building new ones. Wagner changed hands several times, before production ceased in 1970.

Later innovations

All of these machines offered through the 1960s and '70s were of the classic supertractor format: four-wheel drive, an articulated chassis plus a large and very powerful diesel engine. From the

'Delay' mode keeps the rear wheels straight until the fronts have turned 20°, and is designed to aid work with row-crops.

So innovation came thick and fast in the 1980s, despite these being hard times for many farmers and tractor manufacturers while the earlier experiments with tractors of 600hp or more had not made it into the mainstream. It was becoming clear that 500hp was the practical limit. In any case, advances in electronics, both for engine control and cultivation, brought greater efficiency than the quest for ever more power, which brought its own problems of extra weight, cost and bulk. So maybe those 600–900hp giants of the 1970s were just an aberration, the tractor equivalent of American muscle cars that we just won't see again. Maybe these are true dinosaurs of the fields, but the

legacy of the four-wheel-drive, pivot-steer supertractor is firmly established, not just in North America where it originated, but in many other parts of the world as well. One might expect that supertractors have a healthy market in the wide open spaces of Australia and South Africa, and they do, but they are also increasingly used by the relatively smaller farms of Europe. Once again, economics is coming into play. Take the Case Quadtrac STX500, which in 2005 cost £180,000 in Britain. At one time, a tractor of that size would have needed a 1,500-acre farm to justify its cost, but things have changed in the early 21st century. Medium-sized farms are being worked by fewer and fewer people, and supertractors are now viable on lower acreages. Even if the age of the 900hp giants is over, it looks like supertractors are here to stay.

As supertractors have grown bigger, so have their rigid chassis counterparts.

Not that big rear wheels are anything new – this is an American-made Big Four from the 1900s.

John Deere's first successful supertractor was the 7020/7520.

Acknowledgements

Thanks are due to all the people who helped make this book possible, including Peter Love, who searched through his archives for suitable pictures and wrote the foreword; all the tractor owners and collectors for allowing their machines to be photographed; and everyone at Haynes Publishing for taking the whole project on. Special thanks go to my wife Anna for her patience while I stayed up late writing the text.

Bibliography

Ertel, PW, *The American Tractor*, Chrysalis Publishing
Gay, Larry, *Farm Tractors 1975–1995*, ASAE
Gibbard, Stuart, *The Doe Tractor Story*, Old Pond Publishing
Glastonbury, Jim, *The Ultimate Guide to Tractors*, Regency House Publishing
Larsen, Lester, *Farm Tractors 1950–1975*, ASAE
Pakosh, Jarrod, *Versatile Tractors: A Farm Boy's Dream*, Japonica Press
Simpson, Peter et al, *Big Iron in Pictures*, Dieter Theyssen Media
Simpson, Peter et al, *Ultimate Tractor Power* Vols 1 & 2, Japonica Press
Updike, Ken, *International Harvester Tractors 1955–1985*, MBI
Williams, Michael, *Farm Tractors*, Silverdale Books

MAGAZINES
Classic Tractor
Profi International
Tractor & Farming Heritage
Tractor & Machinery

Ready to work? Properly maintained, a supertractor can give 20 or 30 years of reliable service.

AGCOSTAR

Name games

The AGCO story is one of astonishing success and rapid growth. What started out as a low-profile management buy-out of a loss-making manufacturer has grown to become one of the largest tractor concerns in the world, with an annual turnover of more than $3 billion, selling 22 brands in over 8,000 dealers spread across 140 countries. AGCO achieved this, not through long-term development of new tractors and farm machinery, but by buying up respected names when the time was right. The supertractor chapter of this story however, is relatively short.

Launched in 1995, the Cummins-powered 8425 was the first AGCOSTAR.

AGCO would probably never have come into existence had Allis-Chalmers not sold its agricultural arm to Deutz of Germany back in 1985. The German company had a strategy of selling its own tractors in the USA, badged Deutz-Allis, and from 1989 contracted White to build larger machines on its behalf. But the arrangement did not last long. Deutz-Allis was losing money, and the following year, the Germans agreed to a US-based management buy-out led by Robert Ratcliff.

This couldn't have happened at a better time, with the American tractor and machinery market just starting to climb out of a long recession. That same year, Ratcliff's management team bought Gleaner, and AGCO was formed. In

1991, they added Hesston equipment to the list, and going on to acquire the North American distribution rights to Same in 1992 and Massey Ferguson in '93. At the same time, White-New Idea came under the corporate umbrella.

AGCO now had its own tractor making operation, as well as selling both Same and Massey Ferguson in the USA and Canada. However, the whole operation was about to shift up a gear. In 1994, AGCO took over Massey Ferguson, doubling the size of the company overnight. This made it one of the largest tractor manufacturers in the world, with a significant presence in Europe as well as North America. Just four years on from that original management buy-out, it had become a global player.

Supertractors had not played any part in this, with the biggest AGCO-Allis machines being the 9000 series, with up to 191hp output. Built in the old White factory, these rigid-chassis tractors still used Deutz air-cooled engines, though they would soon move over to Detroit Diesel and Cummins power units.

It was not until late 1994 that AGCO finally moved into the supertractor market, buying the McConnell Manufacturing Company of Stamford, Ontario. McConnell's own history of building big tractors was a short one, and in at least one way mirrored that of AGCO. Ward McConnell grew up on a dairy farm in New York State, with the ambition of building his own

The AGCO corporation grew rapidly out of multiple takeovers, and its multiple tractor range reflected this fact.

Above: AGCO rigid chassis tractors, like this DT240, sold well under various badges, but sadly the same was not true of the AGCOSTAR.

Opposite: An 8425 hard at work at a ploughing match. Underneath the new silver bodywork, it had much in common with the original Massey Ferguson 4000 series.

tractor. At first working as an Oliver dealer, he formed McConnell Manufacturing in 1961, producing a variety of farm equipment.

What Ward really wanted was to make tractors, but lacked the resources to develop his own machines from scratch. His first opportunity arrived in 1985, with the purchase of Marshall tractors, the British company that had grown out of Leyland's tractor arm. This did not work out though, and Ward later sold his British investment. His real step up into tractor manufacture came three years later when Massey Ferguson decided to stop producing the 4000, and he was able to buy the rights to build these supertractors in Canada. McConnell upgraded and updated it as the Massey Ferguson 5200 series, launched in 1989 and still sold only through MF dealers, and in MF colours. Two years later, he began selling the same machines under his own name. These bright yellow McConnell Marcs came in 320hp (Marc 900) and 425hp (Marc 1000) form. Both used six-cylinder Detroit Diesel engines with turbos and intercoolers which were mated to a 12-speed manual transmission with four reverse gears.

When AGCO bought McConnell tractors in 1994, it was really taking a direct descendant of the Massey Ferguson line of supertractors, and reuniting it with the rest of the MF range under the same corporate umbrella. Until then,

The AGCOSTAR 8360 was really an 8425 with a derated power unit. These two similar models did not give customers sufficient choice in an increasingly complex market.

From the brave management buyout of the remains of Deutz-Allis, AGCO rapidly grew into a global player in tractors and agricultural machinery.

AGCO's strategy had been to keep the brand names it had acquired – Allis, White and Massey Ferguson all featuring strongly, but it felt that McConnell was not really a well enough known brand, especially outside North America. Nor did it want to reapply the MF badge, aiming to keep that for its small and medium-sized tractor lines.

Therefore, a new badge was created, and that was AGCOSTAR, launching both the name and the tractor in July 1995. It came from a strong line – the Massey Ferguson 4000 and 5200 series, plus the McConnell Marcs – and looked similar to the tractors that preceded it, but the new AGCOSTAR 8425 did have some significant new features. There was new tinwear, to spruce up what would have been quite an elderly looking machine, and the 12-speed transmission was replaced by an 18-speed, with two reverse gears. This had nine speeds in the typical field-working range of three to eight miles per hour.

What did not change was the 12.7-litre Detroit Diesel 60 series engine, still turbo-intercooled and offering 425hp. However, AGCO was well aware that not all farmers had a Detroit Diesel dealer within easy reach, and offered the alternative of a 14-litre Cummins N-14, which offered identical horsepower and was also turbo-intercooled. Both engines had electronic control to optimise fuel consumption. Following the 1980s recession, costs were being scrutinised more closely than ever, and it was no longer enough for supertractors to simply wield brute horsepower they had to be efficient as well.

A year later, the 8425 was joined by the lower-powered 8360, the spiritual successor to the McConnell Marc 900. It shared most components – chassis, transmission, hydraulics, tinwear – with its big brother, and in fact, the only real difference between the two was engine power. Like the 8425, the 8360 AGCOSTAR used the Cummins N-14, although in derated form, giving 360hp at 2,100rpm. What it did not have was the option of the Detroit Diesel, and AGCO took out this option from the 8425 as well in 1998.

The AGCOSTARs were reliable and hard working, with many well-proven components. They had 35° of articulation to give a good turning radius, and offered all the usual advantages of a big supertractor. But for whatever reason, sales were disappointing. Perhaps the brand was just too new and unknown, when so many well-known badges were available. Brand loyalty is important to tractor buyers, so a farmer purchasing a big John Deere 9000 series would often be trading up from a smaller tractor in the same green and yellow livery. There were no earlier, smaller AGCOSTARs, unless you counted the various

An AGCO-Allis 9745, a late model with four-wheel drive and a rigid chassis, but still carrying Allis-Chalmers colours.

AGCO-Allis, Masseys, Sames and Landinis, which were all in different colours and with different histories. The AGCOSTAR certainly had an impressive lineage, but this wasn't obvious from the badge and having just two similar versions presented a very limited range of alternatives.

The end came in 2002, when Caterpillar offered AGCO the rights to build its Challenger rubber-tracked tractor. How could they refuse? Here was the chance to buy into a whole new technology, and expand the company still further. It was a script that could have been written for AGCO, which had always grown by acquisition. So the Challenger MT800 became part of the range, which really spelt the end for AGCOSTAR as there was no need for two high-horsepower supertractors, even if one had rubber tracks and the other wheels. In 2004, there was speculation that AGCO was looking again at the wheeled supertractor market, with a view to launching a successor to the AGCOSTAR. Unless or until that happens, these big silver machines, which were built for only eight years, remain the corporation's only foray into articulated farm tractors.

Specifications

1995 AGCOSTAR 8425

Engine	(1) Detroit Diesel 60 series
	(2) Cummins N14
Engine type	Water-cooled in-line 6
Aspiration	Turbo-aftercooled
Capacity	(1) 12.7 litres
	(2) 14.0 litres
Power @ flywheel	425hp @ 2,100rpm
Transmission	18 x 2, constant mesh

1996 AGCOSTAR 8360

Engine	Cummins N14
Engine type	Water-cooled in-line 6
Aspiration	Turbo-aftercooled
Capacity	14.0 litres
Power @ flywheel	360hp @ 2,100rpm
Transmission	18 x 2, constant mesh

Allis-Chalmers

Short story

The first supertractor to wear the Allis-Chalmers badge was the 440, although it did not last long in production.

Allis-Chalmers looked, on the face of it, to be the perfect American mainstream tractor maker to build a supertractor. Like International, it had a strong history in heavy construction machinery, so knew plenty about big, powerful diesel engines, pivot-steering and four-wheel drive. It had pioneered the use of turbochargers on tractors and was the first with a mainstream two-wheel drive machine that broke the 100hp barrier.

Allis dabbled in four-wheel drive tractors as well. The 'Bull Moose' of 1953 could pull a 65,000lb load at 25mph, and although it was

designed as a tractor-bulldozer for the US Army, it also had the essential elements of a supertractor. Ten years later, the T-16 was intended primarily for industrial use, but Allis-Chalmers did build a few for field work as well, using a turbocharged four-cylinder engine of 5.7 litres. It proved unreliable in the wheat fields, and most were used for sugar cane harvesting.

There were some other attempts at building an in-house four-wheel-drive tractor, but they failed to reach production, and it was not until 1972 that Allis-Chalmers finally dipped a toe into this

rapidly growing market. Even when it was unveiled, the new 440 proved to be no more than a repainted, rebadged Steiger Bearcat, built at Steiger's factory in Fargo, North Dakota. Powered by a 208hp V8, the 440 proved quite a success, establishing A-C in the supertractor market and being exported to Australia as well as doing service in its native wheat fields. It had a 10-speed transmission offering speeds up to 20mph, plus Steiger's patented swinging power divider while a three-point hitch was optional, as was air conditioning for the roomy cab.

This was all very well, and kept Allis-Chalmers dealers happy, but buying in the 440 cut down its profit margin – A-C would get more return by designing its own four-wheel-drive supertractor. And of course, the 440 was never intended as anything more than a stop-gap, giving an A-C answer to International, John Deere and the rest, until its own home-grown machine was ready.

When this was announced in 1975, it was clear that the new 7580 had taken a leaf out of John Deere's book. JD had used many of its existing two-wheel-drive parts to build the four-wheel-drive 7020, launched three years earlier, and the Allis 7580 grew out of exactly the same philosophy. In fact, around three-quarters of its parts came straight out of the 7000 series two-wheel drives, or were upgraded versions.

The engine was an Allis-Chalmers stalwart, the 7.0-litre direct-injection six-cylinder diesel that had been powering A-C's bigger machines for a decade. Turbocharged and intercooled, this produced 222hp at 2,550rpm. That looked like plenty to follow up the Steiger-built 440, and University of Nebraska tests measured it at 186hp

Allis-Chalmers' D21 was the first mainstream two-wheel-drive tractor to break the 100hp barrier.

The 440 was simply a quick means of getting Allis-Chalmers into the supertractor market, a stopgap until its own machine was ready.

The first in-house Allis supertractor was the 7580; a clever use of existing parts cut costs and development time.

at the PTO, with 160hp at the drawbar. The transmission too, was familiar to anyone who had read the specification sheet of the 7000s – Allis's 20-speed Power Director was a well proven piece of kit.

The cab and bodywork also showed a clear family resemblance to the 7000 series, although the 7580 was a classic supertractor in layout, with four-wheel drive through equal-size wheels (duals were a popular option), and full articulation. A draft-sensitive three-point hitch was standard,

A-C followed up the 7580 with the 250hp 8550, using a 12.0-litre turbocharged diesel from one of the company's industrial crawlers.

along with a PTO, and axle widths were adjustable, making the new Allis adaptable for working in a wide variety of crops. In fact, adaptability seemed to be its strong suit, designed as it was for everything from heavy tillage to row crops.

Despite its 200+hp, the 7580 only came in at the bottom end of the Steiger class, and farmers were soon clamouring for more power and Allis-Chalmers' response appeared in 1978 as the 8550. Although based on the same layout as the 7580, this one packed an extra 90hp or so from its 6120T diesel, a 12.0-litre six that was built by A-C itself, and more usually seen in one of the company's construction crawlers. It had two small turbochargers, instead of one large one, which helped explain the purposeful looking twin exhaust stacks.

Again, Nebraska put it through the testing mill, and measured 254hp at the PTO, 224hp at the drawbar. The 8550 was a big tractor, so big, that the testers at the university had difficulty squeezing it into the test lab! Once they had got over that little difficulty, they recorded gear speeds of between 2.0mph and 19.3mph for the 20-speed transmission, which had partial powershift, and was beefed up to cope with all that extra power. Just to put the power gain into perspective, the 8550's three-point hitch could lift 4.4 tons, 1.5 tons more than that of the 7580.

Meanwhile, the 7000 series two-wheel-drive tractors were starting to show their age, and in 1982 Allis-Chalmers replaced them with the 8000. It was a bad time for the company, which closed two major plants and sold off its deep tillage business that year in an effort to stave off bankruptcy. The same changes fed through into the four-wheel drives, the 7580 and 8550 being replaced by the 4W-220 and 4W-305 respectively. The model numbers referred to their engine horsepower, giving a clue that the 7.0-litre and 12.0-litre power units were carried over, little changed.

Some things were new however. The tractors were restyled in line with the new 8000s, and the cab was much more advanced with large rubber mountings, heavy insulation and soundproofing. The 20-speed transmission was still there, and the 4W-220 had 40° articulation and 26° of oscillation.

Specifications

1975 ALLIS-CHALMERS 7580

Engine	Allis-Chalmers 3750
Engine type	Water-cooled in-line 6
Aspiration	Turbo-intercooled
Capacity	7.0 litres
Power @ flywheel	222hp @ 2,550rpm
Power @ PTO	186hp
Transmission	20 x 4, partial powershift
Top speed	18.9mph
Av shipping weight	23,100lb
Fuel capacity	141gal

1982 ALLIS-CHALMERS 4W-305

Engine	Allis-Chalmers 6120T
Engine type	Water-cooled in-line 6
Capacity	12.0 litres
Aspiration	Turbo
Power @ flywheel	305hp @ 2,300rpm
Power @ PTO	250hp
Transmission	20 x 4, partial powershift
Top speed	17.7mph
Av shipping weight	27,100lb
Fuel capacity	167gal

Allis-Chalmers' 7045 rigid of the 1970s. High-powered two-wheel-drive tractors like this would start to encroach on the market of smaller supertractors.

The trouble was, Allis-Chalmers smallest supertractor was being overtaken by events. Farmers were finding that a 170hp 8070 with front-wheel assist (that is, four-wheel drive with small front wheels) could work more efficiently, and cost less to buy. Things were not helped by A-C's own policy of offering front-wheel assist on the 8000 series at no extra cost. Not only that, but the company was under increasing pressure to cut its own costs, so the slow-selling 4W-220 was dropped from the range in 1984.

The following year, Allis-Chalmers finally stopped making tractors altogether, selling its agricultural arm to Deutz. The famous orange machines were now rebadged Deutz-Allis, and even the 4W-305 failed to make it as part of the new owner's long-term plan, as after just a few had been built as Deutz-Allis's, it was dropped from the range. And that was the end of Allis-Chalmers' short supertractor story.

Opposite: The second-generation Allis-Chalmers supertractors were designated the 4W-220 and 4W-305, the former replacing the 7580.

Above: Ultimately, the 4W Allis machines were made obsolete by a new generation of lighter, front-wheel-assist tractors.

Left: The 4W-305 was Allis-Chalmers' final big tractor, and production did not last long after the takeover by Deutz.

Big Bud

Big is beautiful

One of the earliest Big Buds, the HN320, was an uprated version of the first model, the HN250, its 320hp output providing the designation.

There are many candidates in this book for the title of the most powerful tractor in the world; 500–600hp monsters that would appear to be undisputed. But there's one that stands head and shoulders above all of them. The Big Bud 16V-747 might have been a one-off, but its 16-cylinder Detroit Diesel was rated at 740hp and if need be, this could be turned up to (and it

was) 900hp. At the time, no farm tractor had ever commanded so much power – none has since, either.

If John Deere had not signed an agreement with Wagner in 1968, which saw that supertractor pioneer compelled to cease production, then Big Bud probably would not have happened. Willie Hensler ran a successful

Wagner dealership in Havre, Montana, which has always been a good place to sell and service supertractors. Montana, the USA's fourth largest state, boasts endless acres of wheat prairies, among North America's best – wheat making up about three-quarters of the state's income from crops. This has long been a farming state, with farms mushrooming in the 1870s to supply the boom industries of mining and lumber. Even now, after a long agricultural recession, the state has over 23,000 farms, averaging more than 2,500 acres each. These are the sorts of acreages where bigger is better, and if a supertractor can succeed anywhere, it's here.

However, this did not help Willie Hensler when Wagner stopped making supertractors, leaving him with nothing to sell. Hensler could still service and upgrade Wagners for existing customers, but that alone did not make for a long-term business proposition. In any case, Bud Nelson, Willie's business partner and workshop foreman, had other ideas. For many years he had been toying with the idea of a giant, high-horsepower tractor – bigger than the Wagner – that could work the wheat prairies faster than a conventional machine. The disappearance of Wagner, and the continued demand for high-horsepower tractors from local farmers, gave him the opportunity to make this dream a reality.

In the summer of 1969 the pair set up the Northern Manufacturing Company. In honour of the man whose idea they were, the tractors were

named 'Big Bud', and the first series was titled 'HN' for Hensler/Nelson.

Those early Big Buds owed something to the Wagner, and in fact used many Wagner parts that Hensler's dealership still had in stock. Power came from a 280hp Cummins straight-six diesel, rated at 2,100rpm. The new HN-250 looked quite conventional: a four-wheel-drive pivot-steer machine that was different in scale to just about anything else, but was otherwise similar. It had a

From 1976, the KT series represented the second generation of Big Buds, with a roomier cab and more power.

Happy is the group of English tractor enthusiasts visiting the Big Bud works in Montana.

Like almost every other Big Bud, the KT450 used a Cummins power plant, in this case the 18.9-litre 1150.

This is where the Big Buds go to die, a supertractor graveyard where reusable parts are removed.

born of practical experience in working on this type of machine, and which would help Big Bud grow in popularity.

Launched later in 1969, the HN-250 found a ready market among Montana farmers, as well as those further afield. They appreciated its easy servicing and rugged build, and soon, Hensler and Nelson had taken on extra employees, turning out 15 supertractors a year. Meanwhile, as the stock of Wagner components dried up, standard off-the-shelf parts were substituted from Clark (axles) and Fuller (transmissions). With just a few exceptions, Big Bud remained loyal to Cummins as its engine supplier, right through until production ended in 1991.

The HN-250 was big by the standards of the time, but farmers soon began requesting more power, and Big Bud answered with the HN-320 in 1970. Using an uprated version of the same Cummins 14.1-litre six, this offered (as the name suggested) 320hp at 2,100rpm. Three years later, it was joined by the HN-350, and no prizes for guessing the horsepower of that one. All these Series One HN Big Buds used a 12-speed Fuller transmission, which on the HN-350 allowed a top forward speed of 18.4mph.

Later Big Buds were not just about power though, and from 1977 the Series 2 HN-360 came with a tilting Cruiser Cab. As well as offering even better access to the engine and transmission, this was roomier than the old cab, a full 60in wide, and had full carpeting (floor to ceiling, to cut down noise) as well as air conditioning, not to mention a stereo system. The Big Bud might be a working tool, but it was turning into quite a luxurious one!

swinging drawbar and hydraulic spool valves for towed implements, but no three-point hitch or PTO.

There was one significant innovation though, which stemmed from Hensler and Nelson's hard experience in servicing supertractors. The engine, radiator and transmission of the HN were mounted on a skid unit which could be removed from the chassis for easier and quicker servicing and repair. It was the sort of innovation that was

Specification

1969 BIG BUD HN-250

Engine	Cummins NT855 C280
Engine type	Water-cooled in-line 6
Capacity	14.1 litres
Aspiration	Turbo-intercooled
Power @ flywheel	280hp @ 2,100rpm
Transmission	12 x 2
Top speed	16.6mph
Operating weight	34,000lb
Fuel capacity	404gal

Specification

1976 BIG BUD KT-450

Engine	Cummins KT1150
Engine type	Water-cooled in-line 6
Capacity	18.9 litres
Aspiration	Turbo
Power @ flywheel	450hp @ 2,100rpm
Transmission	12 x 2, 6 x 1 powershift option
Top speed	13.3mph
Av shipping weight	58,500lb
Fuel capacity	458gal

Meanwhile, a supertractor power race was in full swing, and not to be outdone by Steiger or Versatile, Big Bud launched the KT series in 1976. This incorporated much of the same philosophy that had succeeded in the HN series: the skid mounted engine and transmission were there, as well as the tilting cab.

The new feature was even greater horsepower, and there the KT was one of the biggest you could buy. The 14.1-litre Cummins was replaced by an

18.9-litre unit, with 450hp at 2,100rpm. This was joined the following year by a KT-400 and KT-525 (the latter intercooled as well as turbocharged). These power ratings of course, could be changed by tweaking the pump setting, which some farmers did. The KT-525 for example, could be turned up to 612hp, simply by changing the pump.

All the KT Big Buds used a 12-speed Fuller Road Range transmission, and for the first time on a Big Bud, there was the option of a

A graphic illustration of the split construction of a pivot-steer supertractor, of which the Big Bud 525/50 was typical.

Triple wheels were a popular option on Big Buds, especially on higher-powered models such as the 525/50.

powershift set-up, this one with six forward speeds and one reverse. Power outputs of over 400hp were starting to cause problems for the manual clutch, so an automatic powershift looked like the only way to go.

The KT-525 in particular took Big Bud tractor power up another notch, and it could pull an 85ft chisel plough. Like every other Big Bud, the KTs were solidly built, to say the least. The main chassis steel plate was ¾in thick, and even that for the fenders was ⅝in. The finish was built to last as well. English restorer Mike Scaife imported a 525/50, and found little rust on his hard-worked 30-year-old tractor, because it had been so well painted at the factory. Engine-wise, the big

Cummins just needed a small repair to a water side-plate, new gaskets and hoses and a full service, before it was ready for work.

By the time the KT series was in production, Big Bud tractors were being built by Ron Harmon, who had a dream of building the world's first 1,000hp tractor, and he almost succeeded.

Mention the Big Bud 16V-747 to any enthusiast of big tractors and watch their reaction. In supertractor terms, this machine has the legendary status of a Ferrari Daytona or a Harley-Davidson XR1000. It was the most powerful tractor ever made. In fact, in just about every dimension, it was giant size. Here was a tractor of 58 tons operating weight that, nearly

Still in regular work when it was photographed, this well-kept 525/50 typifies Big Buds of the later 1970s, early '80s.

30 years after it was built could still drill 80 acres an hour. In every respect, the 747 was and is the biggest supertractor of them all.

The impetus for this monster came from the Rossi brothers, cotton farmers from Bakersfield, California. They were happy with their Big Bud 525, but wanted even more power to increase work rates, and Ron Harmon was happy to oblige. The deal was that they would have the first prototype 747, which Harmon would monitor while building up to full production. In the event, that never happened, although it was certainly Big Bud's intention to make more 747s – they even produced a brochure, which headlined the big tractor as 'Field Artillery'!

Specification

1978 BIG BUD 16V-747

Engine	Detroit Diesel 16V92T
Engine type	Water-cooled V16 two-stroke diesel
Capacity	24.1 litres
Aspiration	Twin turbochargers, aftercooled
Power @ flywheel	760hp @ 1,900rpm (later 900hp)
Transmission	6 x 1, full powershift
Shipping weight	95,000lb
Operating weight	130,000lb
Fuel capacity	850gal

At the heart of the 747 was a Detroit Diesel 16V92T. For the first time, Big Bud abandoned Cummins in favour of this 24.1-litre V16 diesel. With twin turbochargers, it was rated at 760hp at 1,900rpm when first fitted to the 747, although it was capable of being turned up to 1,000hp. While in California, the big Detroiter was turned up to 900hp, still enough to make it the most powerful tractor ever to work a field. Few transmissions were strong enough to handle this sort of power, so Ron Harmon approached the Twin Disc company, which supplied

Looking a little sadder is this retired 525 in the Big Bud yard, a gaping hole where the Cummins engine once sat.

Specification

1979 BIG BUD 525/50 SERIES 3

Engine	Cummins
Engine type	Water-cooled in-line 6
Capacity	18.9 litres
Aspiration	Turbo-intercooled
Power @ flywheel	525hp @ 2,100rpm
Transmission	9x 2, full powershift
Top speed	9.3mph
Av shipping weight	52,000lb
Fuel capacity	458gal

transmissions for heavy construction equipment. Its snappily named TD-61-2609 was a six-speed powershift that could take the 747's prodigious torque and horsepower without wilting. The tyres had to be specially made for the 747 by United of Canada, 35 x 38 duals, bigger than those seen on any other tractor.

Putting all these components together was not as simple as it might seem, as the 747 was too big even for Big Bud's production line. Instead, it sat in one place and was gradually built up as each component was brought in. By January 1978, the 747 was finished, and after astounding farmers and agricultural press at an equipment show, put on a demonstration at the Rossi brothers'

An engine-less, wheel-less 400/30 sits quietly rotting next to a smaller, older International, which puts the Big Bud's size into perspective.

Californian farm. Some said the 747 could never make a practical tractor – it was simply too big and too cumbersome.

But it turned out to be a real working tool. The Rossis needed a tractor for deep tillage, and were using two Caterpillar D-9 crawlers, each towing five-legged rippers, which could work around 15 acres over a ten hour day. The 747 was hooked up to a 15-leg ripper, and went on to cover the same acreage in an hour, at a depth of four feet. So fast did the 747 work, that the ripper legs overheated and bent out of shape, although stronger ones overcame the problem. The other side of this fast working was straight savings in cash – at the end of the second year, said the Rossi's, their $30,000 tractor had paid for itself. After several years work in California, the world's one and only 747 was sold to a Florida farmer, before being shipped back to Montana, where it continues to work.

Meanwhile, the Big Bud factory continued to make tractors that, while not quite in the 747 class, were still among the most powerful on the market. In 1979 the Series 3 tractors were launched – the company that built them having since changed its name from Northern Manufacturing to Big Bud Inc, for the very good reason that everyone now knew what Big Bud meant. Although only offered for three years, the Series 3 Big Buds proved to be the most popular range of all, with 273 (or 265, according to one source) of these giant tractors built and sold.

The range was wider than ever, replacing the HN and KT series in one fell swoop, and covering 320–525hp. Transmission choices were increasingly important, with 12 or 13-speed manual shift units, plus six or nine-speed powershifts. Take all these variations into account, and there were 16 models of Series 3 Big Bud. The company was evidently impressed by Twin Disc's contribution to the 747, as most of these machines used Twin Disc transmissions, with just three using a Fuller Roadranger and one (the 525/84) a Clark unit. The top model was still the 525hp 'Five and a Quarter', although in 1980 this was beaten by the new 650/50. This drew on 747 experience, using a Detroit Diesel V12 of 650hp mated to a Twin Disc six or nine-speed powershift transmission. All Series 3 Big Buds benefited from new styling and more glass for the cab.

Specification

1986 BIG BUD 440 SERIES 4

Engine	Komatsu
Engine type	Water-cooled in-line 6
Capacity	14.8 litres
Aspiration	Turbo-intercooled
Power @ flywheel	440hp
Transmission	12 x 2, full powershift
Top speed	22.4mph
Operating weight	43,600lb
Min turning radius	18.6ft
Fuel capacity	457gal

Despite the improvements, Big Bud could not get away from a few hard facts during the early 1980s. It was a small company in an industry of giants, the demand for supertractors was falling and US farming was facing a serious depression. The company filed for Chapter 11 bankruptcy in 1982, and production ceased, with just the service department kept going.

This wasn't the end of the story however, and Meissner Tractors bought what was left of Big Bud – they were after all, located next door in Havre, and resumed production three years later. The new tractors were called Series 4s, and while the hood and front grille were restyled, under the skin, they were substantially the same as the Series 3s. There were some new engine options, notably using Komatsu, Caterpillar and Deutz units. The Komatsu-powered 700 Series 4 even approached the power of the legendary 747.

But the truth was that Meissner could not take these tractors into series production, and over five years, just 21 Big Buds were built, all of them one-offs built to specific orders. In 1991, even this bespoke production ceased, although Big Bud tractors continue to work hard, and fast, across North America.

The most powerful tractor the world has ever seen: Big Bud's 16V-747 was a one-off, and still impresses today.

One of the best things about giant supertractors is that everyone can get into the picture!

Caterpillar
Crawler breakthrough

Throughout this book, we have attempted to define all supertractors as following the same format: four-wheel drive through equal-sized wheels, mounted on a pivot-steer chassis. However, if there are a few exceptions to this rule, then one of them has to be the Caterpillar Challenger. The rubber-tracked Cats of the 1980s and '90s were not only high-horsepower tractors in their own right, but had a huge influence on the industry, prompting other manufacturers to offer their own such supertractors.

How it all began: Caterpillar pioneered the use of crawler tracks.

Caterpillar of course, had been wedded to the concept of tracks from the very beginning. The company was formed in 1925, the result of a merger between US manufacturers Best and Holt, both of them long-established crawler manufacturers, and fierce rivals. Through the 1920s, '30s and '40s, Caterpillar crawlers sold in small but steady numbers to farmers who had to cope with difficult soils or heavy drawbar loads. How a tractor transfers power to the ground is absolutely central to its working efficiency, and in

heavy, sticky or wet conditions, crawler tracks are far more effective than wheels. So for some farmers, Caterpillars were a better bet than a wheeled John Deere or an International. The company also pioneered the use of diesel power, a good 30 years before this became the dominant power unit among wheeled tractors.

But while Caterpillar continued to offer crawler tractors aimed at farmers through the 1950s and '60s, sales began to drop off. The fact was that crawlers, for all their superior traction in difficult conditions, had plenty of disadvantages as well. On the road, or even on a dry track, they were noisier and slower than a wheeled tractor, capable of little more than walking pace when most tractors could reach 15mph or more. They were uncomfortable too, without the cushioning effect of pneumatic tyres. Steel tracks were maintenance-intensive, needing frequent lubrication, were heavy work to replace, and expensive to buy. Crawlers also cost more than wheeled tractors in the first place.

These disadvantages were brought into sharp relief by the increasingly popularity of four-wheel drive. A tractor thus equipped might not have the ultimate traction of a crawler in the very worst conditions, but it was halfway there, and came with all the comfort and speed benefits of a conventional wheeled tractor.

When mainstream manufacturers in addition to specialists like Steiger and Versatile, began to offer four-wheel drive, it was clear that conventional steel-tracked crawlers could offer little by comparison and agricultural crawler sales dwindled to a trickle. Caterpillar did try to fight back with sealed and lubricated tracks, but that was missing the point – what farmers really wanted was reasonable hauling speed on the road, and greater comfort, something that no steel crawlers could provide.

Caterpillar clearly had its eye on the supertractor market, and studies were made throughout the late 1960s and early '70s with a view to building one of its own with a 270hp prototype completed, with articulated chassis. Surviving pictures show it with both single and dual-wheel set-ups, but in 1977, the prototype was scrapped, after what the company itself described as: 'many fundamental flaws with four-wheel drive technology. Work quickly resumed on track technology with further tests confirming

tracks' superior performance over wheels in traction, compaction, flotation and manoeuvrability and overall efficiency.' (Caterpillar Ag Products)

Given its tremendous well of knowledge of crawlers, many within the company realised that it made more sense to concentrate on what it knew best, than to build a wheeled supertractor that was no better or worse than that of anyone else. The tractor market has tremendous brand loyalty, so for Caterpillar to sell to farmers again,

Although most famous for its tracked machines, Cat also built a limited number of wheeled tractors, such as this D6B.

The D6B was unusual. Most 1960s Caterpillars used steel crawler tracks, then at the limit of their technology.

Specification

1987 CATERPILLAR CHALLENGER 65

Engine	Caterpillar
Engine type	Water-cooled in-line 6
Capacity	11.1 litres
Aspiration	Turbo-intercooled
Power @ engine	285hp @2,100rpm
Power @ PTO	232hp
Transmission	10 x 2, full powershift
Top speed	18.1mph
Av shipping weight	33,200lb

The first Caterpillar Challenger of 1986 had a massive, squared-off appearance, contrasting here with conventional wheeled supertractors.

Caterpillar's big breakthrough was the use of steel-reinforced rubber tracks, in place of conventional steel tracks.

it had to offer a tempting alternative to the regular brands, something that could not be bought elsewhere. When it was finally announced in 1986, the Caterpillar Challenger was exactly that.

What made the Challenger different was Mobil-Trac. It still used crawler tracks, but made of rubber, reinforced with steel cable. Each track was 24.5in wide and had 36 lugs for added traction. Here, said Caterpillar, was the farmers' Holy Grail, which would offer the best points of both wheels and crawler tracks. Like any crawler, the Mobil-

Trac offered a much larger 'footprint' on the ground than the biggest, widest tyre, thus spreading the tractor's weight, increasing flotation and reducing soil compaction. Any crawler can claim the same benefits, but what made the Mobil-Trac different was that its rubber tracks allowed a road speed of up to 18mph, a respectable speed at the time even for a wheeled tractor. It was nothing less than a full-blooded challenge to the supremacy of the high-horsepower wheeled tractor, so what else could they call this revolutionary new machine but 'Challenger'?

Of course, there were sceptics. Rubber tracks could never take high horsepower and high road speeds, they said, and they would wear out prematurely and be costly to replace. Others were

merely cautious, postponing any purchase until the Mobil-Trac had proved itself. In the event, it did just that. Not only did it prove to be reliable in service, but it was so successful that rival manufacturers began to design rubber crawler tracks of their own.

Case-IH and John Deere both launched similar systems, the former with the innovative four-track Quadtrac and the latter with a tracked version of its familiar 8000 series. Caterpillar actually mounted a legal challenge to John Deere, convinced that its patents had been infringed. AGCO got in on the act too, showing a prototype Massey Ferguson 3200 crawler in 1999. Track Marshall in Britain and Marooka in Japan also launched rubber crawlers, and a number of specialists began to offer aftermarket rubber track conversions for wheeled tractors.

This did not mean to say that the Mobil-Trac had swept all before it, and that the Cat Challenger really did represent the best of all possible worlds. It became clear that the argument of tracks versus wheels depended on circumstance. John Deere, the only manufacturer to offer crawlers or tracks, and thus with little to gain by weighting the argument either way, produced a set of guidelines for its customers who could not decide which was best for them. The conclusion was that which was better really depended on a whole host of different factors, including soil type, farm layout, type of implement, and the crop involved.

Bought new, crawler tractors still cost 10–15 per cent more than their wheeled counterparts, so any savings would have to justify that. There was no doubt, according to John Deere, that tracks were more efficient than wheels when pulling an implement through loose soil in a straight line. They also had a clear advantage in wet soils, but on harder soils with a greasy surface, wheels had just as much traction. Tracks were highly manoeuvrable, but less satisfactory on the turn, as one track has to slip, scuffing the soil and crop.

Although there were sceptics, Caterpillar's Mobil-Trac system soon proved to be reliable and effective.

In Europe, the Challenger was later sold as a Claas, in Claas colours, giving the German manufacturer a new line besides its own combines.

Claas Challengers came in a choice of power outputs, just like the Caterpillar original. This is a 75E.

Tread widths were easier to adjust on wheeled tractors, which also fitted into the ridge bottom between crop lines more neatly, and there was superior ground clearance. Tracks don't get punctures, and their replacement cost is little more than that of a set of dual tyres, but there is more maintenance, due to more moving parts. Tracks were thought to give a better ride in the field, able to span bumps and hollows, but worse on the road, with more vibration. The sceptics were at least partly right – tracks do wear faster on the road than do tyres. However, anyone negotiating a narrow country road in a big tractor with duals might appreciate that a tracked tractor would be narrower. And finally, wheeled tractors can approach track performance on some soils, if they are ballasted correctly.

Meanwhile, there were enough buyers out there convinced by the pro-track argument to write out a cheque to Caterpillar, and the Challenger sold steadily through the late 1980s and early '90s. There were signs that for big farmers who could afford to invest the high purchase price, the Challenger could save them money – some found that they could replace three wheeled tractors with two Challengers, and still get the same amount of work done.

The Challenger 35s and 45s underlined Caterpillar's determination to take the mainstream tractor manufacturers head on.

The original Challenger 65 was powered by one of Caterpillar's own six-cylinder diesels, producing 285hp, with 216hp at the drawbar. Encouraged by the reception, Caterpillar

Specification

Specification

1996 CATERPILLAR CHALLENGER 45

Engine make	Caterpillar
Engine type	Water-cooled in-line 6
Capacity	6.6 litres
Aspiration	Turbo-intercooler
Power @ flywheel	242hp @ 2,100rpm
Power @ PTO	194hp
Transmission	16 x 9, full powershift
Top speed	17.8mph

In 1994, Caterpillar followed up the big Challenger with the less-large 35 and 45 models. This 35 is powered by Cat's own 6.6-litre diesel in 210hp form.

One feature of the smaller Challengers, which was essential to compete with wheeled machines, was adjustable track spacing.

extended the range upwards, offering engines of 400+hp. They also later signed an agreement with Claas of Germany, selling Challengers throughout Europe in Claas colours.

The Challenger 65 was a very large, expensive machine, a class above the mainstream wheeled tractors, so in November 1994, Caterpillar unveiled the smaller Challenger 35 and 45, designed to take the mainstream manufacturers head on. They looked sleeker than the rather boxy 65, with an overhanging nose and large rear drive wheel – the 65 had equal-size drive wheels all round.

Power came from Caterpillar's 6.6-litre six-cylinder diesel, in 210hp or 242hp form, with a 16-speed Funck powershift transmission in each case. This was the same transmission used by the Ford 70 series wheeled tractor, and in fact the lift-linkage and hydraulics, cab and computer controls were all shared with the big Ford as well. Interestingly, the Funck had to be strengthened, as the tracked tractor's minimal wheelspin put more strain on the transmission. It was intended that the new, small Challengers would be more suitable for row crop work than the original, so there was a choice of five different track widths (16–32in) which could be spaced 60in to 120in apart.

Initial impressions of the new baby row-crop Challengers were that they worked impressively well, but were expensive. That was confirmed by *Profi* tractor magazine, which tested a Challenger 45 in October 1996. They found that wheel slip was 'practically unheard of' with lower compaction as icing on the cake. The ultra-rapid steering response took some getting used to, although the Challenger could turn around its own centre. They loved the engine, transmission and hydraulics, but did not like the lack of suspension, feeling every bump five times, once for each wheel! They also observed that at £100,000, the 45 still cost far more than the equivalent wheeled tractor. *Profi* concluded that Caterpillar's baby was not as versatile as a wheeled machine either, lacking the comfort and ultimate speed required for haulage work, but as a specialised field tractor, it came highly recommended, even at the price.

The Challenger 35 and 45 had by then already been joined by the 55, which had a 270hp 7.7 litre

diesel. It proved more popular than the two smaller models, being perceived as offering more horsepower per $. This was especially so in Europe, where under the Claas marketing deal, 75 per cent of all row-crop Challengers sold were 55s.

From a technical point of view, Caterpillar's venture into rubber-tracked tractors had been an undoubted success. The Challenger was a genuine step forward in tractor technology, forcing the mainstream manufacturers to respond, yet it was outside the company's core business of construction and mining equipment. Meanwhile, by early 2002, Caterpillar's state-of-the-art factory in DeKalb, Illinois was running at just 20 per cent capacity. So maybe the farming world should not have been quite so surprised as it was when AGCO announced that it was buying the manufacturing rights to the Challenger from Caterpillar. In just three months, production was transferred to AGCO's own plant at Jackson, Minnesota, and the Challenger range was up and running again, as an AGCO product.

Although the tractors were now AGCO Challengers, they were still largely built by Caterpillar, which then sold the parts to AGCO for final assembly. Engine, transmission, the Mobil-Trac units, cab and many other components were all sourced direct from Caterpillar. By this time, the Challenger line up had divided into two basic ranges – MT700 and MT800 – and in 2006 these were still in

A 16-speed Funck powershift transmission was standard on the 35 and 45, although it had to be strengthened to cope with the minimal slippage of the rubber tracks.

Specification

2006 AGCO CHALLENGER MT865B

Engine	Caterpillar ACERT
Engine type	Water-cooled in-line 6
Capacity	18.1 litres
Aspiration	Turbo-aftercooled
Power @ flywheel	510hp @ 2,100rpm
Power @ PTO	425hp
Transmission	16 x 4, full powershift
Top speed	24.6mph
Av shipping weight	42,200lb
Fuel capacity	330gal (US)

every bump five times as a new Opti-ride suspension system used rubber and fabric springs to allow each track to oscillate independently of the other. The mid wheels were suspended as well.

The MT800B had all the same advances, with the addition of more power, and lots of it. The power units were still a Caterpillar exclusive, this

Challengers could be tricky to drive for anyone used to a conventional tractor, as the tracks gave an ultra-sharp steering response.

Challenger was the right name for Caterpillar's bold venture into the agricultural tractor market as it forced the established manufacturers to sit up and take notice.

production, with a 'B' suffix to denote the most recent update. The baby Challengers had been left far behind, to concentrate on the high-horsepower sector.

The MT700B was powered by a 9.0-litre (537ci) Caterpillar C9 ACERT engine, with three models offering 270hp, 300hp or 320hp respectively, all rated at 2,100rpm. AGCO claimed that the latest MT700 was 2dB quieter than the old one, with an air-suspended seat and sophisticated ventilation system to keep the driver happy. Things had changed since *Profi* magazine found that five wheels in each track meant feeling

time the ACERT series that was described as all new by AGCO. With electronic injection, lower emissions and lighter fuel consumption, these were state-of-the-art diesels. The range kicked off with the MT835B (350hp), followed by the MT845B (400hp) and MT855B (460hp), all of which used Caterpillar's 15.2-litre ACERT engine.

A bigger, 18.1-litre unit was used for the MT865B (510hp) and range-topping MT875B (570hp), which incidentally, AGCO claimed to be the highest-horsepower mass-produced tractor in the world. Not a bad sign-off for Caterpillar, which even if it no longer assembled the leading rubber-tracked tractor, still appeared to build a large proportion of it.

Ultimately, Caterpillar decided to pull out of tractor making, but the Challenger lived on as part of the AGCO range.

CNH Global

Multiple heritage

CNH Global is one of the largest farm equipment builders in the world, although like AGCO, it is the result of several acquisitions – the genes of Case, International Harvester, New Holland, Ford, Fiat and Steiger are all detectable in this giant corporation. After the merger of Case-IH and New Holland in 1999, it had combined revenues of $11 billion – there had never been a tractor maker this big before.

Case remains a key element to the company, and it has the deepest roots – Jerome Increase

The first supertractor from Case, the 1200 Traction King. Smaller than a Steiger, it was still a big machine; the driver lends scale.

Case began making threshers in Racine, Wisconsin, in 1843. He progressed to big steam engines, something the Case tractor philosophy would reflect for decades to come. The Case way was to build big, heavy, strong and under stressed, and the company only reluctantly built a lightweight rival to the small Farmall F-12 in the 1930s.

The first Case prototype of the 1890s was a heavy, 30hp machine, intended for threshing work. It came to nothing, but when Case finally

went into production in 1916, it was with the famous Crossmotor range, so called because the four-cylinder engine was mounted across the frame. Although the smaller Crossmotors sold well, Case's heart was in the giant 40-72 version, with its 20.0-litre four-cylinder engine and ability to pull a 12-furrow plough.

If Case had a flaw, it was that innovation tended to come in bursts rather than at a steady rate and by the time the Crossmotor was replaced by the solid Model L in 1929, it was seriously out of date. The company had failed to come up with a rapid response to the all-round versatility of the Farmall and John Deere C in the 1930s. Eagle Hitch, its answer to the three-point hitch of Ford's 9N, came ten years later, and without draft control. In the early 1950s, it offered no diesel option, live power take-off or power steering while its big tractors were still chain-driven.

But in the late 1950s, Case had another one of its periodic bursts of innovation, this time playing catch-up with a new diesel, eight-speed transmission (with optional torque converter Case-O-Matic), gear drive and a three-point hitch with draft control. Pushed through by energetic new Vice President Marc Rojtman (although they had been in development before his arrival) this tidal wave of new features cost a lot of cash to develop. In fact, this R&D spending spree was to drive Case into a takeover

by Tenneco Inc in 1967, but at least it had a modern range of tractors to sell in the meantime.

What it lacked in the early 1960s was an answer to the new breed of four-wheel-drive supertractors. Not just from Steiger and Wagner, but the tentative offerings from John Deere and International as well. When it appeared in 1964, the Case contender was unveiled as the 1200 Traction King, and what a title to conjure with that was, as evocative in its own way as the Steiger brothers' fondness for big cat names.

It was quite a different concept to the machines that had inspired it. John Deere's 8010

A decade later, the Traction King name was carried by the Case 2670, now with a standard cab and a 12-speed powershift transmission.

Just like its predecessors, the 2670 used a rigid chassis and four-wheel steering instead of the pivot-steer system favoured by other manufacturers.

Specification

1964 CASE 1200 TRACTION KING

Engine	Case
Engine type	Water-cooled in-line 6
Capacity	7.4 litres
Aspiration	Turbo
Power @ PTO	120hp @ 2,000rpm
Power @ drawbar	107hp
Transmission	Eight-speed, constant mesh
Top speed	14.1mph
Operating weight	16,585lb

Long past its best, a 2670 Traction King sits in a yard, awaiting rebuild or scrapping. The line established Case as a supertractor manufacturer.

Hard at work with sugar cane, this Case-International is one of the new generation of pivot-steer Cases.

offered more than 200hp, and the Steiger and International supertractors, 300hp or more. The Traction King was smaller than any of its rivals, with a relatively puny 120hp at 2,000rpm. The engine was an existing Case unit, a 7.4-litre six-cylinder diesel with the addition of a turbocharger and oil cooler.

Instead of using a pivot-steer chassis, as would most supertractors, the Traction King's frame was rigid, but it did offer four-wheel steering for a tighter turn. The rear axle could be locked in a straight-ahead position, co-ordinate with the

front wheels automatically, or turn in the same direction, giving crab steering. Crab steering was especially useful, allowing the machine to safely traverse steep hillsides and reduce soil compaction, as the rear wheels did not follow in the tracks of the front pair. Using hydraulics front and rear, the system worked well, and enabled the chunky Traction King to claim a turning radius of 16.5ft, despite its four big, equal-sized wheels.

Case's first supertractor had further selling points too. Unlike other big machines, it had a conventional three-point hitch, so could use existing implements. It also had vacuum-assisted hydraulic brakes all round and an eight-speed

constant-mesh transmission. The Traction King proved a success, and 1,549 of them were sold over a four-year production, making it quite a big seller in supertractor terms.

So successful was the 1200 Traction King that its 1969 successor followed the same lines. Announced the same year as the takeover by Tenneco, the Traction King 1470 had, like its predecessor, a rigid frame and hydraulic four-wheel steering. The braking system was changed to a caliper disc brake on the main drive line, instead of being wheel mounted, and the new tractor came with a cab as standard – Case having

pioneered factory-fitted cabs in the early 1960s.

Naturally, there was more power, although Case continued to fit one of its own diesel engines instead of shopping for a big Cummins or Caterpillar unit. The 8.3-litre engine was the first of a new generation of direct injection diesels developed in-house by Case. It would be a mainstay of the Case tractor range for many years, and turbocharged in the Traction King, it gave 145hp at 2,000rpm, driving through an eight-speed transmission, as before.

Two years later, the 1470 was joined by the powered up 2470, with the 8.3 litre turbo-diesel

A joint venture with Cummins produced the CDC-Case engine range, which powered many Case supertractors through the 1990s.

Below: Case or Steiger? After initially selling Steiger tractors with Case badges, the company responded to public demand and returned to the Steiger badge.

Bottom: This 9370 wasn't the flagship Case supertractor of the mid-1990s, that was the 425hp 9390.

Opposite: The Quadtrac was Case-IH's response to the Caterpillar Challenger.

now delivering 174hp at the PTO, according to the University of Nebraska, and 154hp at the drawbar, both at the rated 2,200rpm. But the real advance came in the new 12-speed transmission. Equipped with partial power shifting, to allow clutchless changes between ranges on the move, this gave speeds of 2–15mph.

Move on another three years, to 1974, and many manufacturers were using intercoolers to squeeze more power out of turbocharged diesels. The principle was a simple one: cooling down the incoming charge air (either with an air-to-air or water-to-air intercooler) reduced its volume and made it more dense, thus packing more air into each cylinder. With the fuelling turned up to suit, this made for a bigger burn and more power. In the case of the new 2670 Traction King, this

Specification

1980 CASE 4890

Engine	Saab-Scania
Engine type	Water-cooled in-line 6
Capacity	11.1 litres
Aspiration	Turbo
Power @ PTO	253hp @ 2,200rpm
Power @ drawbar	225hp
Transmission	12-speed, partial powershift
Top speed	18.2mph
Operating weight	25,750lb

boosted outputs to 219hp at the PTO and 193hp at the drawbar. A higher powered 2870 would soon join the range as well, although this time, Case opted to buy in an engine from truck maker Saab-Scania, an 11.1-litre turbocharged unit that offered over 250hp at the PTO.

Otherwise, the 2670 used the same 12-speed partial powershift transmission as the 2470, giving speeds of up to 14.5mph. The four-wheel steering system was still there and the Case Traction King continued to offer a more compact alternative to some of the bigger supertractors. Its colour scheme had changed, from the traditional Case desert sunset to white and red, reflecting the colours of British manufacturer David Brown, which was bought by Case in 1974.

The 70 series Traction King range was replaced in 1980 by the 90 series, although in truth, this remained more of an update than anything more radical. In fact, the power units were unchanged for the new 4490, 4690 and 4890, which replaced the 2470, 2670 and 2870 respectively, and retained the 12-speed partial powershift transmission as well.

There was revised styling and a new four-post roll-over protection cab, which also reduced the interior noise level to 78dB(A). One significant advance was the addition of electronic sensors to the four-wheel steering, which allowed for more sensitive control. Steering modes could now be selected on the move simply by flicking a rocker switch on the console. Apart from that, the system was still based on two separate hydraulic circuits for the front and rear axles. All three 90 series tractors were tested by the University of Nebraska

The Quadtrac was quite different from the Caterpillar Challenger, using four independent tracks and a pivot-steer chassis.

in the year of their release. The 4490 recorded 175hp at the PTO, 153hp at the drawbar; the 4690 220hp/196hp, and the 4890 253hp/225hp.

Since takeover by Tenneco, Case had been on a firmer financial footing than ever before, something which enabled it to weather the storms of the early 1980s far better than its arch-rival International. In fact, Tenneco would swallow International as well in 1985, forcing a merger of the two tractor lines.

The year before, the 90 series supertractors were given a final update as the 94 series. Once again, there were no big changes, with power outputs, transmission and four-wheel steering all being carried over. The new line-up of 4494, 4694 and 4894 continued in production until the end of the decade.

The 4994 was the biggest, most powerful tractor ever launched by Case. It was based on the same four-wheel steering as its smaller

The Quadtrac concept lived on in the STX series that replaced it; there was still no supertractor like it.

brothers, but moved up into the high-horsepower class. Case had no suitable engine for such a tractor, and so turned to Saab-Scania once more, this time choosing a 14.2 litre V8 offering 400hp at the flywheel. In the 4994, this translated into 344hp at the PTO and still just over 300hp at the drawbar. Once again, transmission was the 12-speed partial powershift. In tests, it proved to be the most efficient of all four Case supertractors, with a top fuel figure of 17.03hp-hr/gallon.

However, formidable as the 4994 was, it had a relatively short career. It also marked the limits of Case's four-wheel steering layout, which could not handle very high outputs, and looked outdated next to the latest pivot-steer machines. After the merger with International, there was naturally a period of rationalisation, and the 94 series four-wheel drives were chosen to wear the new Case-IH badge, instead of International's own range of supertractors.

This included the 4994, but in 1987 Tenneco made another acquisition, and this time it was the turn of Steiger to seek the shelter of this big corporate umbrella. There obviously wasn't room for two competing supertractors in the same company, which spelt the end for the 4994 in favour of the well-established Steigers, although the smaller, four-wheel-drive 94s carried on to

1989/90, and two updated four-wheel steer tractors, the 9240 and 9260, were built through to 1993. So while Steiger supertractors continued to roll out of the factory in Fargo, North Dakota, they were soon rebadged as Case-IH machines, and came in the new corporate colours of red and black.

To the horror of Steiger lovers everywhere, not only was their famous badge consigned to the rubbish bin, but so were the big cat names that had graced Steigers since the very beginning. In their place came a more logical (but less inspiring) series of numbers as favoured by Case-IH. The Steiger Puma, Bearcat, Cougar, Panther and Lion were replaced by the Case-IH 9110, 9130, 9150, 9170 and 9180 respectively. Steiger's high-powered Kp 525 became the 9190.

Heartless perhaps, but this gave Case-IH an established range of well-proven and respected supertractors, with decades of know-how behind them. It was also a complete line up, ranging from the 200hp and 220hp 9110/9130 (both already powered by Case diesel engines), up to the 375hp 9180 and 525hp 9190, both with Cummins power. The two smallest tractors came with variable wheel spacing from 60 to 130 inches, making them suitable for row-crop work. In an interesting variation on the pivot-steer theme, they also had a steering front axle, which

Alongside the supertractors, Case also offered a wide range of four-wheel-drive rigid-chassis machines, such as this MX270.

The four wheeled STX model numbers referred to their horsepower; this an STX450.

for the updated 9300 series, but this did not happen until 1995.

In the meantime, the updated 9200 series was launched, in August 1990. The big, 500+hp model was dropped, while the five-model 9210-9280 range covered engine power figures of 200hp to 375hp. Engine suppliers were unchanged, the 9210 and 9230 still using Case (now CDC, a joint project between Case and Cummins) units, and the more powerful 9250, 9270 and 9280 sticking with Cummins. One new feature across the range was the Skip-Shift transmission, which allowed the driver to shift directly from 1st gear to 4th, and from 6th to 8th. It was a recognition that for road haulage, or even when using lighter implements in the field, not all twelve ratios in the 12-speed powershift were needed – missing out a couple on the way through the system saved time. Another new transmission feature was the addition of a third reverse gear, enabling the big 9200s to rocket backwards at up to 8mph.

could turn up to 6° in either direction before the pivot-steering kicked in. This allowed for fine row-crop adjustments without full articulation.

But there was a snag. Case-IH's hasty dropping of the Steiger name had not gone down well in an industry where history counted for much and brand loyalty for even more. Steiger was the biggest name in supertractors, worldwide, and killing this valuable brand name was, with hindsight, a serious mistake. To its credit though, Case-IH recognised this, and revived the name

Case-IH had been marketing its final four-wheel steer tractors, the 9240 and 9260, as its biggest row-crop machines, but when these were dropped in 1993, their place was taken by a row-crop variant of the pivot-steerers. The 9250 RCS (Row-Crop Special) had an independently steerable front axle as well as full articulation,

The STX line-up looked new, but carried over many updated features from its predecessor, the 9300, such as Autoskip shifting. This is an STX500. It might have been sold in Case colours, but the STX represented a sum of supertractor know-how, from Steiger and Versatile as well as Case and New Holland.

Specification

1987 CASE-IH 9110

Engine	CDC-Case
Engine type	Water-cooled in-line 6
Capacity	8.3 litres
Aspiration	Turbo
Power @ flywheel	200hp @ 2,100rpm
Power @ PTO	168hp
Transmission	12-speed, full powershift
Top speed	16.5mph
Operating weight	20,160lb
Min turning radius	12.8ft
Fuel capacity	96gal

with up to 18° available in total. By selecting front axle steer, or articulation, or a combination of the two, the driver could place the tractor very

accurately, minimising damage to crops. With the front axle turned as tightly as it would go, together with full articulation, the 9250 could turn in a radius of just 12.2ft, making this the most manoeuvrable supertractor of its time.

The concept was evidently a popular one, for when the updated 9300 series was launched in 1995 (complete with Steiger badge sitting proudly on the front grille) the Row Crop Special option was extended to three models. The 9310 (205hp), 9330 (240hp), and 9350 (310hp) all came in either Standard or RCS form. The larger 9300s did not have the row-crop option, but did offer more power than their predecessors, in the case of the top 9390, 425hp at 2,100rpm, or 383hp at the PTO. Supertractor power was creeping up once again, as the farmers began to seek more ways to speed up work and cut their fixed costs.

Transmission options had blossomed since the days of the early Case four-wheel steerers. Buyers

Something else carried over from the 9300 was the Quadtrac system, and it remained a unique solution to the wheels versus tracks debate.

Specification

1997 CASE-IH 9390 STEIGER

Engine	Cummins N14-A400
Engine type	Water-cooled in-line 6
Capacity	14.0 litres
Aspiration	Turbo-intercooled
Power @ flywheel	425hp @ 2,100rpm
Power @ PTO	383hp
Transmission	12 x 3 Syncroshift, 24 x 6 optional
Top speed	17.7mph
Operating weight	44,000lb
Fuel capacity	225gal

The biggest tractor ever made? CNH used this eye-catching air-filled New Holland at agricultural shows all over the country.

This was the supertractor New Holland brought to CNH Global, the 82 Series descended from the original Versatile line.

of the two lowest powered 9300s were offered a 12-speed full powershift unit, with three reverse speeds. Move up to the 9350, 9370 and 9380, and there were three transmissions to choose from. Standard was the 12 x 3 Syncroshift, although you could have that with a hi-lo range as well, giving 24 x 6 ratios and a top forward speed of 19mph. Finally, the 12 x 3 set-up could be had as a powershift. Buyers of the 425hp 9390 had just two options, the 12 x 3 Syncroshift and its hi-lo equivalent.

Even before the 9300 series was launched, Case-IH had been experimenting with a new concept in supertractor design. Inspired by the Caterpillar Challenger, it used rubber crawler tracks, but unlike Caterpillar or John Deere, which used two tracks either side of a rigid chassis, the Case-IH 'EXP' used four smaller ones, keeping the pivot-steer frames. There had been four-track machines before, but never from a mainstream manufacturer.

Finally launched in 1997 as the Quadtrac, Case-IH's latest supertractor combined the advantages of a crawler (traction, minimal ground

pressure) with those of a pivot-steer wheeled tractor (maintaining traction under a powered turn). Naturally, the Quadtrac was not quite as tight turning as the wheeled equivalent, but it could manage a radius of 19.5 feet, combined with a ground pressure of just 5psi. Each track had a 'footprint' of over 2,000 square inches.

Unlike a rigid crawler, the Quadtrac could turn under load, as it did not need to skid one track to make the turn. Slippage was a minimal 2–3 per cent, compared with 12–16 per cent for a wheeled supertractor, and the Quadtrac could still thunder along the tarmac at up to 19mph, making it at least as fast as its wheeled rivals. To keep the tracks in contact with the ground, all four pivoted up and down independently. Two models of Quadtrac were offered, the 360hp 9370 and 400hp 9380.

A good guide as to how successful a concept has been is whether it reappears when the range is updated. On that criterion, the Quadtrac qualifies, as in 2000 when the 9300 Case-IHs were replaced by the STX range, the Quadtrac came too. By this time of course, Case-IH formed part of the giant CNH Global concern, formed by the merger between Case-IH and New Holland.

New Holland had its own range of supertractors, descended from the Ford Versatile line. These had been replaced in 1994 with the 80 series, and ranged from the 250hp 9280 to

the 9880 of 400hp. All were conventional, wheeled pivot-steer machines, with a new 12-speed Quadra-Sync transmission which had powershift across three ranges of four speeds. The 80 series retained some of their Versatile ancestry, such as relatively light weight and the use of 'C' channel steel for the chassis, instead of flat steel.

The tractors were rebadged New Holland in 1997, along with an upgrade to the 82 series, with power outputs now spanning 260–425hp, while the Quadra-Sync was retained. Two years later, another upgrade saw the 84 series unveiled with two models – 9184 and 9384 – replacing the 260hp 9282. This was the supertractor range

Specification

2001 NEW HOLLAND TJ440

Engine	Cummins QSX15
Engine type	Water-cooled in-line 6
Aspiration	Turbo-intercooled
Power @ flywheel	440hp @ 2,000rpm
Transmission	16 x 2, full powershift
Top speed	23mph
Operating weight	52,800lb
Min turning radius	16.7ft
Fuel capacity	250gal

Not exactly a supertractor, but Versatile's innovative bi-directional concept lived on as the New Holland TV140.

New Holland 82 Series supertractors did not survive the CNH merger for long. Just two years later it was replaced by this, the TJ series. This is a TJ450 which used the same choice of CDC or Cummins power units and 16-speed powershift transmission.

Despite the New Holland badges and colours, the TJ series was really a repainted Case STX – the economics of a multi-national concern. This is a TJ375.

New Holland brought to CNH in 1999, and for the first few years, this series was offered alongside the big Case-IH machines. Rationalisation dictated that when the time came for a new range, these two separate line ups would be replaced by one.

The Case-IH STX was also sold in New Holland blue/black as the TJ series. They were otherwise very similar, using the same range of CDC or Cummins power units and 16-speed powershift, although New Holland customers did not have a Quadtrac option.

Meanwhile, the red/black Case-IH STX was CNH's first high-horsepower tractor launch after the merger – it being unveiled in 2000, a year before the TJ series. The basic line-up was of four models, the numbers in each case referring to engine horsepower, including the CDC-powered STX275 and STX325, and the Cummins-powered STX375 and STX440. Many of the features of the earlier tractors reappeared in updated or renamed form. So Autoskip was a development of Skip-Shift, allowing the driver to skip every other ratio right up to the top road speed of 23mph, and save time in the process. AccuSteer was descended from the combination of front axle and pivot-steering, which had first appeared back in the late 1980s. As before, it enabled far more accurate steering, just what was needed for delicate tip-toeing between rows of crops. The top power STX440 claimed up to 43 per cent torque rise, and all the STX tractors drove through a 16-speed full powershift

transmission. Of course, there was the Quadtrac, an option on the STX375 and STX440.

CNH Global headed into the 21st century, a giant of the industry which, along the way, had swallowed the two most famous names in supertractor history – Steiger and Versatile.

Specification
2000 CASE-IH STX375 QUADTRAC
Engine	Cummins QSX15
Engine type	Water-cooled in-line 6
Aspiration	Turbo-intercooled
Power @ flywheel	375hp @ 2,000rpm
Power @ PTO	311hp
Transmission	16-speed full powershift
Top speed	23mph
Operating weight	53,264lb
Min turning radius	18.6ft
Fuel capacity	300gal

New Holland's flagship for the 21st century, the 500hp TJ500. It was only available in wheeled form, and the Quadtrac concept remained an exclusive Case preserve.

Doe

English eccentric?

Perhaps the best-known tandem tractor in Europe, possibly the world, the Doe Triple-D was an English take on the supertractor concept.

Ernest Doe & Sons was not the only company in the world to build a four-wheel-drive tractor by connecting two conventional machines in tandem, but it is probably still the best known. The idea is simple in theory, hitching up a couple of, say, 50hp two-wheel-drive tractors to produce a 100hp four-wheel drive with pivot-steering. Several conversion kits have been offered over the years, and in the USA, Ford actually went into limited production with a semi-tandem hitch, which it claimed could be fitted in less than 90 minutes. Of course, as soon as other specialists began offering their high-horsepower single-unit

four-wheel drives, tandems like the Doe Triple-D began to look unwieldy, complex and expensive, but for few years in the 1960s they filled a gap in the market for affordable four-wheel drive with relatively high power.

Although Doe is universally remembered as the maker of tandem tractors, it did not invent the concept. In 1957, Essex farmer George Pryor needed a new machine to replace his County crawler. The County had traction enough to cope with the farm's heavy clay soil, but George found it too slow. A 100hp wheeled tractor would be ideal, except that in 1957 no such thing existed

in England. So he hit on the idea of connecting two Fordson Diesel Majors together with a steel beam. Traction was still lacking, but removing the two tractors' front axles, and using a swivelling turntable to connect them, effectively turned them into a single, four-wheel-drive 104hp machine.

The prototype was built over the winter of 1957/58, just as the Steiger brothers were building their own four-wheel-drive supertractor, thousands of miles away across the Atlantic. Field trials of the Pryor tandem showed great promise. Although over 20ft long, it was highly manoeuvrable, and at 21ft, the turning radius was actually 5ft less than that of a standard Fordson Major. It could pull twice as much as the County crawler, and more than twice as fast.

Not surprisingly, the Pryor tandem created a lot of interest, and long-established agricultural dealer Ernest Doe, a friend of George Pryor, offered to put it into production. A few changes were made, such as replacing the steering tiller with a conventional wheel, although the process

of changing gear was still a little unusual. Selection between high, low and neutral ranges could be made from the seat on the rear unit, via a series of linkage rods. With the front tractor in neutral range, the driver had to dismount from his seat on the rear unit, walk round to the front, select gear on the main range, walk back, select high or low (plus the same gear combination on the rear unit) and only then could he drive off. It was a complicated arrangement, but it worked, although production had to be suspended after a few months on the orders of Health and Safety

The badges say it all. Although based on two Fordson Super Majors, the Doe was a fully patented tractor in its own right.

One of the Triple-D's advantages over a conventional tractor was its manoeuvrability. Despite being 20ft long, its turning circle was just 21ft.

Right: In the field, the Triple-D offered four-wheel drive and over 100hp, which made it unique in 1960s Britain.

Opposite: As its Fordson Super Major base unit was updated, so was the Doe, but a new breed of rigid four-wheel-drive tractors was to make it obsolete.

With an experienced driver at the helm, a Doe was highly effective, but its vague steering and idiosyncratic gear selection could catch out the unwary.

officials. They were concerned that if the linkage rods were worn, it would be difficult to tell whether the front unit really was in neutral. Doe developed a new system, allowing remote hydraulic operation of the front unit transmission, and production of the Doe Triple-D restarted in May 1960.

Even with the new arrangement, Triple-D drivers needed some time to acclimatise themselves. It was still possible to set front and rear units in two different gear ratios, or even one in forward and the other in reverse! There was potential for expensive transmission damage, although the tractor would often simply stall before gear teeth began shearing. Steering took some getting used to as well. Even when new, the 20ft long Triple-D required a certain finesse at the wheel, but as the hydraulic ram wore, steering became increasingly erratic, especially on the road. Add in the difficulty of pulling out of blind junctions, preceded by that long nose, and it was clear that the big Doe required an experienced driver!

At £1,950, the Triple-D was not a cheap tractor by the standards of the time, but a 93hp Caterpillar D6 crawler cost close to an astronomical £7,000, and was far more expensive to run. Not only that, but the Doe could work much faster as well. One Triple-D completed a 12-hour ploughing marathon, working over 30 acres, which came out at 2.57 acres an hour, using just 1.19 gallons of diesel per acre. The economics of this embryo supertractor were clear for all to see.

As the basic Fordson tractor was updated, so was the Doe. From the end of 1960 it was based on the new Super Major, which brought disc brakes, a differential lock and draft control hydraulics. Because no-one else was offering anything quite like the Triple-D, Doe of Essex was kept busy building tandem tractors for export all over the world. Triple-Ds were sold throughout Europe, as well as Russia, Israel and various parts of Africa. Some were even shipped across the Atlantic to North America, where South Dakotan farmer Ralph Christensen (who had already built his own Ford-based tandem) acted as agent. He named it the Double T, but unfortunately was only able to sell three before pressure of other work forced him to pull out.

The Triple-D was updated again in the summer of 1963 and was now based on the New Performance Super Major Fordson, and with power boosted to 108hp. Production was higher than ever, and demand was so strong that Doe was planning to erect a bigger factory. However, the fact remained that the Triple-D could not

Below: The Triple-D was by no means the world's only tandem tractor, and others have been built as specialist, high-power machines. This is a Chamberlain from Australia.

Specification

1963 DOE TRIPLE-D

Engine	Fordson
Engine type	Water-cooled in-line 4
Capacity	2 x 3.6 litres
Power @ PTO	108hp
Transmission	Six-speed
Av shipping weight	11,000lb approx.

The Doe 130 was a logical successor to the Triple-D and was based on the D5000, Ford's replacement for the Super Major.

exist without its Fordson skid units and in 1964, Ford ceased production of its long-serving tractor in favour of the all-new integrated range. This was therefore the end of the Triple-D.

Fortunately, as a well-established Ford dealer, Doe received an early preview of the new range in October 1964. So it just had time to prepare a tandem tractor based on the flagship Ford 5000, in time for the Smithfield Show in December. With several years experience of the Triple-D behind them, Doe engineers were able to build the new Doe 130 in double quick time.

However, they had to fabricate new subframes, a new cast-steel turntable and develop hydrostatic steering.

The Ford 5000 was a big advance on the old Super Major, with 65hp and an eight-speed transmission. This translated into 130hp for the twin-engined Doe 130, which was fitted with a heavy-duty, 13in clutch, in place of the standard 12in version. One new feature that did not translate well was the optional 10-speed Select-O-Speed transmission, which allowed clutchless changes on the move. It proved jerky in

ballast to counteract the weight of the implement being towed also reduced rear tyre wear.

Historically, Doe rear units had a harder time than those at the front. They drove the hydraulics and power steering, and many farmers switched the front engine off for road work, to save fuel. To equalise effort in the field. Doe set the front unit to run 150–200rpm faster than the rear, making life easier for the rear by a 'pulling' it through.

Idiosyncrasies like these, though they could be surmounted, began to count against the Doe. By 1968, farmers had a choice of specialist four-wheel-drive tractors from County, Roadless and Dutra, offering similar horsepower to the Doe at a lower price. Being single-unit tractors, they were more compact, easier to drive and used less fuel. That year, Ford updated the 5000 as part of the new Ford Force range, and which was now 75hp.

Doe did the obvious thing, and built a Triple-D 150 based on this latest tractor, advertising it as, 'Better, Quicker, Cheaper,' but only three were sold, and the company decided to cease production. It had never made a big profit on its tandem tractors, and made the decision to concentrate on its thriving business as a Ford dealer. It later offered the Doe 5100, a 98hp six-cylinder conversion of the 5000, but this was soon withdrawn at Ford's request. The legacy of the Doe Triple-D is clear: a unique 100hp four-wheel-drive tractor that was like nothing else at the time.

This home-built Oliver tandem was later split up and rebuilt as two separate tractors.

operation, and with the two units' gear selectors connected by cable, it was difficult to be sure that both were in the same ratio. Only a single 130 was sold with Select-O-Speed.

Like its predecessor, the 130 proved an immediate success, with 73 sold in the first year alone. Once again, it was one of the most powerful tractors on the market, so powerful that it could shred the six-ply 12 x 38 tyres which were fitted as standard. Specifying the optional eight-ply tyres (an extra £40) cured the problem, while it was found that increasing front-end

Ford FW

Better late …

Ford was a latecomer to the world of supertractors, which is a little puzzling. After all, here was an American tractor pioneer which, apart from a 10-year hiatus in the 1930s, had been building farm tractors in the USA since 1917. It had plenty of experience with powerful cars and trucks, while the Ford corporation had a record of spotting market niches, and even creating new ones.

But as supertractor sales gathered momentum in the 1960s and early '70s, Ford showed no sign of joining in, although all of their competitors did. Steiger, Wagner and Versatile were the established specialists, while in 1959/60, John Deere and International dipped their toes into the four-wheel drive market. Case followed soon afterwards, and Oliver/Minneapolis-Moline in 1969. In '72, both Allis-Chalmers and Massey

If Ford didn't make a supertractor, you could always hot-rod your old Fordson. This V8 is a home-brewed special.

Ferguson entered the fray. Meanwhile Ford seemed content with offering ever more powerful two-wheel-drive machines, but leaving articulated supertractors to everyone else.

It was not until 1977 that a supertractor with the Ford badge finally appeared, and even then it took the well-worn path of buying someone else's machine and repainting it to suit a different set of dealers. So the new Ford FW series announced that year were really Steigers, with some mostly minor changes in specification which Ford asked for. Steiger of course, was no stranger to this badge engineering, and had already built four-wheel-drive tractors for Allis-Chalmers and International, as well as Canadian Co-op Implements.

The advantage for Ford was that they were able to offer a complete range of supertractors from the start, each one based on a well proven Steiger. These were the 210hp FW-20, based on the Steiger Bearcat, the 265hp FW-30 and 295hp FW-40 (both based on Steiger's Cougar) and the 335hp FW-60, based on the Steiger Panther.

Not surprisingly, despite the Ford colours, all of these looked very similar to the Series III Steigers from which they originated, but under the bodywork there was a substantial difference. Instead of the straight-six Cummins favoured by Steiger, Ford opted for a Cummins V8, using the 9.1-litre V-555 in the FW-20, with all other models powered by the much larger 14.8-litre V8. In the case of the flagship FW-60, a turbo was added.

All of them used a split torque 10-speed transmission, with the option of a two-speed transfer case giving 20 forward speeds and four reverse. They also had the option of a three-point hitch, while the standard lift capacity was 5.7 tons.

Ford might have little track record in this market, but it did have the advantage of a huge spread of dealers across the world, and FWs were soon being exported to Europe and Australia as well as parts of Asia and the Middle East. The FW-30 was launched in Britain in the autumn of 1978, its big brother, the FW-60, following two years later. In fact, the big Fords found more

Another modified Ford, this time with massive twin wheels. Ford's lack of an in-house supertractor encouraged such ingenuity.

Yet another alternative was to opt for a four-wheel-drive rigid, such as this 4000-Four. Still no supertractor from Ford though.

Specification

1977 FORD FW-30

Engine	Cummins
Engine type	Water-cooled V8
Capacity	14.8 litres
Power @ flywheel	265hp @ 2,600rpm
Power @ PTO	205hp
Transmission	10 x 2 (20 x 4 opt)
Top speed	22mph
Operating weight	32,000lb
Fuel capacity	187gal

Ford was late in entering the supertractor market, and even then, the FW series was simply a rebadged Steiger.

All FWs were Cummins-powered; in the case of the FW-60 by a 14.8-litre turbocharged V8 of 335hp.

success in Europe than they did at home. In North America, the lime-green Steigers were so well established as the supertractor of choice that there was little reason to buy one with a Ford badge, unless there was a dealer nearby. The situation was reversed in Europe, where Steigers were very rare, but blue and white Ford tractors were already a familiar sight. The V8-powered Ford FW series were certainly impressive performers, but sales in North America were disappointing.

According to one source, Ford actually dropped the FW-20 and FW-30 as early as 1980, in the face of increasing sales of the front-wheel assist TW series; another maintains that it was the FW-40 that was first go. Whatever the truth, what is certain is that in 1982 Ford stopped selling any FWs in North America. But, such was its success in Europe that Steigers in Ford colours continued to cross the Atlantic. The FW-30 was given a power boost for the Europeans, to match the 295hp of the old FW-40, and in 1984 the FW-60 was revamped with a 14.1-litre turbocharged and aftercooled six-cylinder engine

(Cummins of course), offering 325hp at
2,100rpm. Twenty years later, some of these
Euro-specification FWs could still be found, hard
at work.

These Steiger-based tractors were only part of
the Ford FW story and on the other side of the
world, a similar deal was done between Ford
Australia and Waltanna, the supertractor
specialist from Down Under. Waltanna built two
prototypes in 1985, and the FW-25 and FW-35
announced the following year used engines from
Ford's own 163hp TW-25 and 195hp TW-35.
They were soon joined by another five Australian
FWs, ranging from 280hp to 400hp, all powered
by Caterpillar turbocharged diesels. These were of
course, completely unrelated to the Steiger-built
FWs that were popular in Europe. In any case,
the Waltanna connection was a short one, as in
1987, Ford New Holland bought out Versatile.
This meant a new in-house source of
supertractors, which spelt the end for the
Waltanna-made machines.

Ford's farm equipment arm had become Ford
New Holland in 1985, after taking over the
agricultural machinery specialist. Two years later,
the purchase of Versatile brought a new
generation of four-wheel-drive supertractors
under the corporate umbrella. At first, the

Versatile Designation 6 tractors resumed
production in their traditional red and yellow,
but in late 1988, they swapped to Ford colours
and badging, although the Versatile name still
appeared in small script.

The Ford-Versatile range of five tractors (846,
876, 946, 976 and 1156) was well respected, and
they were relatively light in weight for such large
machines, thanks in part to the use of 'C' channel
steel for the chassis, instead of flat plate. There

The top-of-the-range Ford-Versatile, the 1156, is seen here with twin wheels.

Ford New Holland launched the 80 Series to replace the Designation 6s in 1994, although the Ford badge was soon dropped.

How it all began – the Fordson F. Little did Henry Ford know that his first Fordson would lead to those giants of the wheat prairies.

Buying-in a supertractor actually made sense for Ford. It was quicker and cheaper than developing its own design for what was still a relatively limited market. There were four models of FW based on Steiger's Bearcat, Cougar and Panther, but some detail changes were requested by Ford.

were some changes, with slight power alterations and the option of a 12-speed powershift transmission, while other alterations, such as a Category III three-point hitch and 1,000rpm PTO, were aimed at the European export market, where the Ford-Versatile Designation 6s replaced Ford's Steiger-built FW series.

Meanwhile, Ford New Holland was working hard on a replacement for the ex-Versatile machines, which would eventually be launched as the 80 series in 1994. Corporate machinations of the time had seen Fiat take over Ford New Holland, agreeing to use the Ford name on tractors up until the year 2000 only.

Specification

1989 FORD-VERSATILE 946

Engine	Cummins NTA-855
Engine type	Water-cooled in-line 6
Capacity	14.1 litres
Aspiration	Turbo-aftercooled
Power @ flywheel	325hp @ 2,100rpm
Power @ PTO	286hp
Transmission	12 x 4 constant mesh, 12 x 2 powershift option
Top speed	15.2mph
Operating weight	32,500lb
Fuel capacity	238gal

Nevertheless, for three years, the new 80 series was badged as a Ford tractor, in the familiar blue colour scheme, and even kept the small script Versatile badge as a reminder of its heritage.

The four-strong 80 series range spanned 250–400hp, the lowest powered 9280 using a Cummins LT10-A, with the 9480, 9680 and 9880 all sharing the same company's NTA 14.1-litre six, in 300hp, 350hp or 400hp tune

respectively. All four tractors used a 12-speed Quadra-Sync transmission as standard, with a 12-speed powershift optional on the middle two. In 1997, all were replaced by the updated 82 series, and as the previous year Ford New Holland had decided to drop the Ford part of its name, these were badged as New Hollands only. That was the end of the Ford supertractor story, which involved tractors built by Steiger, Versatile and Waltanna, but none by Ford itself.

Many 1950s Fordsons were converted to four-wheel drive by specialists such as County and Roadless.

Try getting one of these without four-wheel drive! The Ford-Versatile 82 Series line-up.

International

'Snoopy' and friends

International built high-horsepower two-wheel-drive rigids as well as supertractors. This is a 1466 Turbo, with 145hp at the PTO.

International Harvester is one of the oldest names in the North American tractor industry, the result of a 1902 merger between McCormick, Deering and three smaller concerns. Surviving some internecine warfare between Deering and McCormick (prior to the merger, they had been arch-rivals), the new corporation thrived. It made its name with the relatively lightweight Mogul and Titan tractors in the 1910s, then really hit the big time with the Farmall in 1924. This was the first tractor strong enough for belt work, yet nimble enough to work row crops. It was a huge success, but sadly, this did not last, and from the early 1960s, International entered a slow decline, which culminated in its being taken over by Tenneco, the owner of Case, in 1985.

However, International certainly was not backward in developing supertractors, and compared with some of its mainstream rivals was quite proactive. While others were prepared to buy rebadged Steigers or Versatiles, International bought into Steiger and built the 66 and 86

Specification

1965 INTERNATIONAL 4100

Engine	International Harvester
Engine type	Water-cooled in-line 6
Capacity	7.1 litres
Aspiration	Turbo
Power @ PTO	140hp @ 2,400rpm
Power @ drawbar	125hp
Transmission	Eight-speed constant mesh
Top speed	20.25mph
Operating weight	15,175lb

Series as a joint project. When the company was finally taken over, it was offering the distinctive 2+2 – the 'Snoopy'.

Like John Deere, International had dipped its toe in the supertractor market with an in-house design well before the sales boom of the early 1970s. Announced in 1960 (the year after John Deere's own 8010), the International 4300 made quite an impact. It was the most powerful diesel farm tractor anyone had ever seen, with 300hp on tap. Just to put that in perspective, the Steiger brothers' first home-built machine offered 238hp, and John Deere's 8010, just 215hp. Only Wagner, which had been in the supertractor business longer than anyone, could equal it, with the 300hp TR24.

Wagners of course, were more often used in the construction industry than in farming, and the same proved to be true of the 4300. It clearly owed more to construction machinery than any existing tractor, and was even built by International's Hough Industrial Division, rather than by the agricultural side of the company.

So everything about the 4300 was on a different scale to what farmers were used to. Power came from International's own 13.4-litre turbocharged straight-six, which made over 200hp available at the drawbar. There was power steering and an eight-speed selective transmission, air brakes (another sign of industrial, rather than farming, heritage) and planetary reduction axles. A cab was optional, but there was no PTO, and the whole thing weighed nearly 15 tons – no wonder it needed those air brakes!

All this hardware had the potential to make a formidable monster for the Mid West prairies. The 4300 could pull field cultivators 45 and even 60 feet wide, and International made a special 10-furrow plough to suit it. But this very scale proved a barrier to the tractor's acceptance – it was just so far from what farmers were used to. Only 44 4300s were built between 1960 and 1963 (one source says 1965), and most of those were bought for construction work, rather than farming.

International's next stab at building a supertractor was a little more successful, and certainly on a more familiar scale. Announced in 1965, the International 4100 was still built by Hough Industrial, but it had evidently been designed with farmers in mind. The engine was little more than half the size of the 4300's, a 7.1-litre turbocharged six that claimed 140hp at the PTO, and 125hp at the drawbar.

Smaller and lighter than its predecessor, the 4100 used a pure tractor transmission, borrowing

The 4166 was quite compact by supertractor standards, and suited far more farmers than did the massive 4300.

International's 4366 was a genuine joint venture with Steiger. Built at Fargo it had a Steiger chassis and cab with International engine and transmission.

This bonnetless 4366 is something of a hybrid, having been fitted with a later, 86 Series, cab.

gearbox and range units from International's biggest two-wheel drive tractors, the 806/1206. The operator could flick between four-wheel drive in the field and two-wheel drive on the road, while a 1,000rpm PTO was optional, so unlike the 4300, this latest International could drive implements as well. The chassis was not articulated, but the front axle did have an oscillation feature that allowed it to follow undulations in the ground – not quite as sophisticated as the independent front suspension on some of today's tractors, but quite advanced for its time.

As on the 4300, a cab was optional, but this one also had tinted glass and opening windows, along with the further options of heating and air conditioning. The seat was mounted on rubber springs and an oil-filled shock absorber to give the driver as smooth a ride as possible. There were even neat little details like a fold-out toolbox beneath one of the steps. By supertractor standards of the time, the 4100 sold quite well too, with 1,217 finding homes between 1966 and 1968. It was replaced in '69 by the 4156, although this was little changed apart from the badges, and only 218 were sold in its final two years.

There is a story behind the drop-off in 4156 sales. The supertractor market was developing fast, and International's entrant was looking increasingly outdated by the early 1970s. They replaced it, but the 4166 announced in 1972, was

still no attempt to out-muscle Steiger or Versatile. Instead, IH sought to repeat the trick of the 4100, offering a small, four-wheel-drive tractor of less than 150hp. Half a class down from the Steigers, the new 4166 offered four-wheel drive traction at just over $30,000, saving nearly $20,000 on the price of a full-size supertractor.

Oddly, despite its truck and industrial divisions, with their own expertise in high-horsepower machinery, International chose to look for a partner when designing the 4166. It settled on Mississippi Road Supply (MRS), agreeing a joint venture in late 1970 to build a whole range of four-wheel-drive tractors. The company already had a link with MRS, which had been converting International W9s and WD9s into earth-moving equipment since the 1940s. The plan was that MRS would build the tractors, while International would use its considerable corporate muscle to provide financial stability, marketing and distribution.

There were to be four supertractors in the MRS/International line up, all to enter production in February 1971, and all based on existing MRS machines. The model A-60 was to be rebadged and repainted as an International 4166, the A-75 as the 4168, the A-80 as the

4266, and the A-100 as the 4366. The two smaller machines would swap to IH power units (a DT-466 for the 4166). There were also plans for an IH 4468, based on MRS's projected A-105, due for launch in the summer of 1971. A three-year contract was signed, and everything looked good.

But it never happened. It is still not known why the agreement between International and MRS was abandoned so rapidly. This left IH with the problem of finding a new partner – it had already decided that designing and building its own in-house supertractor would be prohibitively expensive, but wanted to have more engineering involvement than a simple repaint/rebadge job. With MRS out of the window, they went straight to the top and took a 28 per cent stake in Steiger.

It made sense for both parties – International gained access to a well-proven production facility with a wealth of supertractor know-how, while little Steiger received a very welcome injection of hard cash, plus the chance to sell tractors through IH's extensive dealer network.

When the 4366 was finally announced in 1973, it soon became clear that this was the result of a genuine joint venture – there was no question of International dealers being asked to sell a badge-

By 1977, the International four-wheel drives had become the four-model 86 Series range. This intercooled 4386 had been joined by the V8-powered 4586 and 4786, and a derated 4186.

engineered Steiger. The articulated chassis was built by Steiger, with 40° of articulation allowing a tight, 15ft turning radius. The cab was Steiger's own as well, the Fargo firm's existing Safari cab, painted in IH colours and had rubber Isomounts to minimise vibration, with extra insulation to keep engine noise and heat away from the driver. As well as comprehensive instrumentation, the cab was pressurised with filtered air, and had the option of air conditioning and a whole list of different radios.

Steiger of course, did not build engines, so IH delivered its own DT-466 to Fargo. This 7.7-litre turbocharged six-cylinder diesel claimed 225hp at 2,600rpm, with almost 170hp available at the drawbar. The transmission was a combination of in-house and bought-in parts, with a Fuller five-speed unit mated to a two-speed transfer box, giving ten forward speeds in all, and two reverse. Axles were borrowed from International's 1466 two-wheel drive, although that at the rear did without the differential lock and brakes. Both were pressure-lubricated and cooled, and allowed the choice of single or twin-wheel set-ups. The transfer case was a 'swinging' type, which moved in the same direction as the tractor, putting less strain on universal joints.

All in all, the 4366 proved to be a highly successful hybrid, combining the best of Steiger's expertise with International's distribution

A 4386 with its Steiger cousins. Production of these supertractors soldiered on into the 1980s, by which time they were starting to look a little outdated.

Specification

1973 INTERNATIONAL 4366

Engine	International Harvester
Engine type	Water-cooled in-line 6
Capacity	7.7 litres
Aspiration	Turbo
Power @ flywheel	225hp @ 2,600rpm
Power @ PTO	168hp
Transmission	10 x 2 constant mesh
Top speed	20.5mph
Av shipping weight	19,500lb
Fuel capacity	118gal

channels and off-the-shelf parts. Tested by the University of Nebraska (the US standard for tractor testing) in 1973, it offered gear speeds of 2.5mph to 20.5mph, and tipped the scales at 21,690lb. The weight was well distributed, as with a rear implement in place, it gave an ideal 50/50. A Steiger-designed three-point hitch was optional. Over 3,000 4366s were sold in three years, and IH must have judged its rapidly formed alliance with Steiger a great success.

This encouraged them to add a powered-up version of the tractor in 1975, and the 4568 made use of International's V-800 engine. The name came from its capacity of almost 800 cubic

Specification

1979 INTERNATIONAL 4786

Engine	International Harvester DV-800
Engine type	Water-cooled V8
Capacity	13.2 litres
Aspiration	Turbo
Power @ flywheel	350hp @ 2,600rpm
Power @ drawbar	265hp
Transmission	10 x 2 constant mesh
Top speed	18.2mph
Av shipping weight	23,600lb
Fuel capacity	162gal

inches (13.2 litres) which could muster 300hp; 857 of these tractors were sold in 1975–76.

By the time those final 4568s had rolled off the Steiger production line, International had already launched its 86 Pro-Ag series, which updated its entire tractor line-up in one fell swoop. The four-wheel drives had the same treatment, with paint and decals to fit in with the new look, but it wasn't just a cosmetic job. The renamed 4386 gained an intercooler, the first to be used on an IH farm tractor, and along with the 4586, a new brake set-up. These were wet, multiple disc, externally mounted stoppers, which were needed

to cope with the extra power of the 4386. The cab (still designed and built by Steiger) was larger than before, and now incorporated the IH data centre, a digital readout in place of a conventional tachometer, which could show engine rpm, travel speed and exhaust gas temperature. Two-speed wipers and an AM-FM radio completed the package.

Although the International four-wheel drives had been conceived as half a class down from the full-size Steigers, their power ratings were creeping upwards. The two existing tractors were joined by a new 4786, this fitted with a turbocharged version of International's DV-800, offering 350hp, with 265hp at the drawbar. Nebraska tested this one in 1979, recording speeds of 1.8–16.1mph, and fuel efficiency of 11.92hp-hr/gal. At the other end of the scale, a 4186 was added to the range, with 150hp from International's smaller 7.2-litre six, still turbocharged.

Brakes and intercooler apart, the 4386 and 4586 were mechanically unchanged from their predecessors, and soldiered on in production to 1981, as did their smaller and larger brothers. The plan was to replace these with an updated 88 Series – the 7388, 7588 and 7788 – restyled to match the latest smaller Internationals. Sadly, the company was in dire financial straits by this time, and only two examples were built, both 7788s.

'Snoopy', the 'Anteater', call it what you will, the International 2+2 was a unique supertractor.

To bring in some cash, International sold its stake in Steiger to the Deutz Corporation, while IH dealers were given leave to sell Steigers instead, so they at least had a supertractor to offer, even if it wore the wrong badge.

By then of course, the giant Steiger-Internationals were starting to look a little elderly, it having been nearly a decade since their introduction. International Harvester had a radically different four-wheel drive under development well before then, and in 1979, this was unveiled.

To American farmers, it was the 'Anteater'; British and Australian farmers knew it as 'Snoopy'. Others favoured the name 'Worm' or 'Land Shark', while International Harvester preferred the more prosaic '2+2'. Either way, International's last supertractor, before the company was taken over by Case in 1985, was a unique piece of design. There had been nothing like it before, and at the time of writing, there's been nothing like it since.

You can see how the long-nosed 'Snoopy' got its nickname, but the model did not figure in the plans of the newly merged Case-International.

Specification

1979 INTERNATIONAL 2+2 3588

Engine	International Harvester DT-466B
Engine type	Water-cooled in-line 6
Capacity	7.7 litres
Aspiration	Turbo
Power @ flywheel	200hp @ 2,500rpm
Power @ PTO	170hp
Transmission	12 x 6
Top speed	17.7mph
Av shipping weight	17,000lb
Min turning radius	15.9ft
Fuel capacity	127gal

It was back in 1970 when IH engineers mated two final drives from the two-wheel-drive 1066 tractor, to build a four-wheel-drive machine. The idea was not to build a replacement for the big 4166, but to design something of 130–150hp that would slot in between International's two-wheel-drive models and the true supertractors. To maximise economies of scale, it would use as many two-wheel drive components as possible.

Development of this odd-looking tractor continued through the 1970s. The engineers decided to mount the cab behind the articulation joint, rather than in front as in the layout of every other supertractor. This was the masterstroke that made the 2+2 unique, underlining IH's claim that it had two-wheel drive manoeuvrability and handling, along with four-wheel drive traction. This appeared to be borne out in practice, with a turning radius of just under 16ft, something which many conventional tractors could not match.

To keep a good portion of the weight over the front wheels, the engine was mounted well forward, over the front axle, giving 'Snoopy' that distinctive nose, plus excellent weight distribution. Another advantage of the layout was that the cab and rear-end of a two-wheel-drive 1086 Series International could be used complete, with little modification to the drive train. Naturally, power came from existing IH six-cylinder diesels, with the 3388 2+2 using the DT-436 unit with 157hp. Farmers needing more power could opt for the 177hp 3588, which was

fitted with a 7.7-litre unit. These were joined in 1980, by the 200hp 3788.

After their 1979 unveiling, the 'Snoopys' caused a sensation. They looked like nothing else, a real hybrid between a two-wheel-drive row-crop and a supertractor. They performed well too, with good traction from the four equal-sized wheels, and fine flotation. While the cab view looked similar to that of a conventional 86 Series, the driving experience was quite different – the tractor was pulled in the direction of its nose, and there was a short time-lag between the nose turning and the tail following. Steering also proved quite sensitive, especially on the road, but the 2+2 proved highly manoeuvrable, its tight turning radius reducing or eliminating the need for headland shunting. Drivers just had to be aware of that long nose when pulling out into traffic.

Despite their unusual layout, the 55 series 'Snoopys' proved a hit with American farmers, who bought nearly 3,000 in the first two years. It was a real boost for International, still on the financial slide that would lead to its takeover. The 2+2 proved relatively trouble-free in service too, although the closed centre hydraulic system (which only ran when needed, to save fuel) could fail completely, knocking out the steering as well as the main hydraulics. An expensive new pump solved the problem. A side effect of that tight turning was that fitting dual wheels to the front could actually result in them hitting the cab, so IH specified that duals should be fitted to the rear only.

Specification

1982 INTERNATIONAL 6388

Engine	International Harvester DT-436B
Engine type	Water-cooled in-line 6
Capacity	7.2 litres
Aspiration	Turbo
Power @ flywheel	157hp @ 2,400rpm
Power @ PTO	131hp
Transmission	16 x 8
Top speed	20.7mph
Av shipping weight	16,340lb
Min turning radius	15.9ft
Fuel capacity	127gal

All three 2+2s were updated as the 60 Series (6388, 6588 and 6788) in 1982, which brought new paintwork and decals, in line with the smaller Internationals. There were changes under the skin too. A hydraulic transmission brake operated automatically, making for smoother, easier shifting between ranges. In the Control Center Cab, the major controls were grouped on the right-hand console while IH's digital data centre was still standard.

Unfortunately, despite the 2+2's good points, its reputation had suffered from those earlier hydraulic failures, while the 3788 tractor had final-drive problems. Coupled with the farming slump in the USA, and IH's own mounting debt, these troubles saw little more than 1,000 of the facelifted 60 series 'Snoopys' built over three years. It remains a rare and collectable supertractor.

If all had gone according to plan, that would not have been the end of the 'Snoopy' story. International designed a 7288 and 7488, taking the 2+2 over the 200hp mark at the PTO, with a completely redesigned drivetrain because of the extra power. Only 35 of these Super 70 Series 2+2s were finally sold, before the Case takeover put a premature end to production of International's final supertractor. Half-finished tractors on the production line were scrapped – a sad end for a unique machine.

Placing the cab behind the pivot-steer joint, instead of in front, gave the 'Snoopy' superb manoeuvrability with a turning circle of 16ft.

JCB
Speed records

Below: The Fastrac was a milestone in tractor technology, combining all-round suspension with powerful brakes and a 40mph road speed.

Opposite: JCB wanted to make the Fastrac a usable tractor in the field as well, although it was inevitably a compromise compared with a conventional tractor.

Towards the end of the 20th century, the idea that a British company could not only design and build a revolutionary new tractor, but achieve worldwide success in the process, seemed like a pipedream. At the time, tractor makers all over the globe, including those which had survived the difficult years of the 1980s, were finding things hard enough, and the industry was rife with mergers and takeovers.

Meanwhile, the British manufacturing industry had been in steady decline for over 50 years, and two major tractor plants – the ex-International factory in Doncaster and Massey Ferguson in

Coventry – had been sold to new owners. The MF plant, once one of the largest tractor factories in the world, actually closed in 2002.

Against this background, the groundbreaking design of the JCB Fastrac made a huge impact, with success in export markets across the world, as icing on the cake. The company itself was something of a quiet success story. Joe Bamford had set up in business in Uttoxeter in 1945, having famously bought an electric welding set for £1. His first product was a farm trailer, built mainly out of scrap and an old Jeep axle. He soon progressed to hydraulic tipping trailers,

With the 1100 series (this is an 1135) JCB sought to make the Fastrac more field-friendly than the original model.

The ultimate solution to the Fastrac's lack of manoeuvrability was the Quadtronic four-wheel steering system, which was expensive, but very effective.

which in turn led to hydraulic loaders designed for tractors. On a sales trip to Norway, he spotted a hydraulic backhoe, brought one home and designed his own version. With one of those and a front loader attached to a Fordson Major, the famous JCB 'digger' was born. It was a runaway success, and thousands were made, increasingly sophisticated as the years went by. By 1995, JCB was building more than 18,000 machines a year, and in 2006 employed 5,000 people.

Joe Bamford had started out making equipment for farmers, but the success of the digger had overshadowed that market for a long

time. Fast forward to the 1980s, when JCB's market research had pinpointed an interesting gap in the farm tractor market. Most tractors were designed primarily with field work in mind – road haulage was seen as a minor activity. Yet JCB's research revealed that throughout Europe transportation was a highly significant part of the workload of many tractors, in some cases up to 70 per cent. Conventional tractors of the time, limited to perhaps 20mph, with rigid axles and poor brakes, were quite unsuited to road haulage, which on a large modern farm could involve a trip of many miles. JCB engineers reasoned that a

high-speed tractor with suspension and powerful brakes would make a much better job of the haulage role.

There had been high-speed tractors before of course. The 1970s Trantor was one, and Mercedes' ubiquitous Unimog another, but the Trantor was a low-production machine, and the Unimog was more truck than tractor. If a Unimog was 80 per cent truck, 20 per cent tractor, and a conventional tractor the other way round, then JCB's project would aim to be 50/50, a genuine dual-purpose machine that could haul at reasonable speeds on the road, and do a good job in the field as well.

By 1987, the first prototype was running, incorporating all those key features which would make JCB's first agricultural tractor unique. When the Fastrac was finally launched in 1991, it was this combination that worked. First and most obvious, the transmission enabled a speed of 40–45mph on the road, about twice as fast as a conventional tractor. Such speeds would have been suicidal with conventional suspension and brakes, and the Fastrac was the first high-draft tractor with full suspension. Coil springs and telescopic shock absorbers were fitted at the front, with a hydro-pneumatic self-levelling system at the rear. Self-levelling was essential to keep the rear ride height constant, regardless of the weight

Specification

1996 JCB FASTRAC 1135 QUADTRONIC

Engine	Perkins 1006-6T
Engine type	Water-cooled in-line 6
Capacity	6.0 litres
Aspiration	Turbo
Power @ flywheel	135hp @ 2,400rpm
Torque	406lb ft
Transmission	36 x 12 Selectronic
Top speed	30mph
Av shipping weight	11,660lb
Fuel capacity	48gal

being carried on the rear linkage or load platform. Conventional rear suspension would have made it very difficult to control the draft on ploughs and other implements. Four-wheel disc brakes were fitted, to keep the speed in check. To make the Fastrac into a credible field tractor, it had four-wheel-drive through equal-sized wheels, a heavy-duty three-point linkage that could handle a five-furrow reversible plough, a front linkage, and front and rear PTOs.

Here was a tractor that could haul a 14-tonne load at normal traffic speeds, in safety. It could

Early buyers wanted more power, and JCB responded with the Fastrac 185, complete with 170hp Cummins turbo-intercooled six.

The Fastrac had a major revamp in 1998 as the 2000/3000 series; this is the 2135.

The 2135 remained the lead-in model, still powered by Perkins and still not cheap either, but the Fastrac remained a unique supertractor.

More-rounded styling brought the 2000 series Fastrac out of its 1980s design roots, among many other changes.

The Fastrac influenced mainstream tractor manufacturers to redesign their own suspension systems, but none of them sought to challenge JCB head on.

carry 2.5 tonnes on the rear load deck as well, and work the fields like a conventional tractor. The surprising thing was that one feature intended to make the Fastrac a safe, high-speed tractor on the road – the suspension – also paid dividends in the field. The Agricultural Development and Advisory Service (ADAS) made a performance comparison between the Fastrac and a conventional tractor, and found that the JCB worked up to 30 per cent faster in some secondary cultivation jobs. So it was hardly a surprise when the mainstream tractor makers began to fit suspension systems in the years that followed the Fastrac's launch.

Initially, the Fastrac came in just two versions – the 120 and the 145 – both powered by Perkins diesel engines, but despite the limited range it met with immediate success, selling particularly well in Germany. Two years later, these were updated as the 120–150hp 125, 135 and 150, all using the latest Perkins 1000 series high-torque rise six-cylinder engines. Some farmers wanted still more power of course, and the following year JCB responded with the Fastrac 185. There was no suitable Perkins power plant, so for the first time the company bought in a Cummins engine, a turbo-intercooled six of 170hp. Transmission and rear axle were uprated to cope with the extra power, but otherwise the 185 used the same Powersplit transmission as other Fastracs, with 36 forward and 12 reverse gears.

Of course, the Fastrac wasn't perfect, and one glaring drawback of its four equal-sized wheels and rigid chassis was a lack of manoeuvrability. In fact, the consensus was that the early Fastrac was biased more towards road haulage, leaving it compromised in the field, especially compared with a conventional tractor. JCB sought to address this in 1995 with the 1100 series. The new 1115 and 1135 were 150mm shorter and 100mm narrower than the existing machine, lighter in weight and with a road speed of 30mph instead of 40mph. It all added up to a 21ft turning radius, which was better, but still not quite up to conventional standards. JCB's answer came the following year.

Quadtronic was a four-wheel-steering system, which for the first time, made the Fastrac as manoeuvrable as some of the most nimble conventional tractors. The rear wheels could turn up to 20° (half the articulation of the front pair) and the system was sophisticated enough to offer five different modes. Conventional two-wheel steer was intended for the road, with the rear axle locked in a straight position. Crab steer pointed all wheels in the same direction; proportional tracking (the rear wheels moved 1° for ever 2° of front turn) gave the tightest turning; true tracking saw all wheels turn by the same amount, and 'delay' meant no rear-wheel steer until the front wheels were at 15°, allowing adjustments without the rear kicking out.

The Quadtronic system worked very well, although at £5,700 extra, it wasn't cheap. Now several years old, the Fastrac is a well-known niche tractor, although its reliability isn't the best, put down to a combination of build quality and driver abuse. In 1998, the 2000/3000 series brought a whole raft of changes, including more-rounded styling and an electronic dashboard. Perhaps the most significant change was the addition of a three-speed powershift to the six-speed Eaton gearbox and Selectronic system. Add up all the combinations, and this can offer 54 forward speeds and 12 reverse, with 30–40mph speeds on the road. JCB had worked hard to give the Fastrac a more field-friendly transmission, and the 54-speed unit was the result. In 2000, this had another upgrade with the Smoothshift electro-hydraulic clutch, a wet multi-plate unit which was smoother, lighter and stronger than dry single-plate system it replaced. Electronic control made it less susceptible to abuse, and allowed a push-button control for shuttling between forward and reverse.

Ten years on from its launch, the Fastrac was still the only tractor with all-round suspension, offering unrivalled driver comfort and on-road behaviour. Without the expensive Quadtronic option however, it was still less manoeuvrable than a conventional tractor, and the transmission was another limiting factor, as was the power limit of 170hp.

By 2005, JCB had addressed two of these concerns with the substantially new Fastrac 8250. Here was the most powerful Fastrac yet, with a 248hp Cummins engine, an 8.3-litre turbo-intercooled unit with 870lb ft of torque. Perhaps even bigger news was the V-Tronic CVT fully automatic transmission. This used internals from the German Fendt CVT, with JCB input/output shafts and electronics. It was a state-of-the-art

A more sophisticated transmission was another advance that came with the 2000/3000 series with up to 54 speeds offered.

Continuous development was essential, and the Fastrac gained a tougher multi-plate wet clutch in the year 2000. This is a 3220.

As ever, customers wanted more power, and this 3220 was the flagship, at least for a while. It was later superseded by the 248hp 8250.

Perhaps not a major seller on a global scale, but the Fastrac did well for JCB, filling its own market niche better than any rival.

Above: Was this the inspiration for the Fastrac? Perhaps, but the long-running Mercedes Unimog was more truck than tractor.

Opposite: Not just farmers appreciated the Fastrac, as this military fleet order demonstrates.

system, with various modes allowing fully automatic, manual or powershift choices in the ranges 0–30mph or 0–40mph. New axles and the biggest tyres ever seen on a Fastrac also helped endow the 8250 with better field performance than ever before.

This latest Fastrac was proclaimed as the best yet, and the one most likely to attract mainstream farms to buy a JCB instead of a conventional tractor. After a decade and a half in production, the Fastrac is still a niche product, but its legacy is that of a revolutionary high-speed tractor that changed industry thinking about suspension and on-road speeds.

Specification

2005 JCB FASTRAC 8250

Engine	Cummins QSC
Engine type	Water-cooled in-line 6
Capacity	8.3 litres
Aspiration	Turbo-intercooled
Power @ flywheel	248hp
Torque	870lb ft
Transmission	Two-range CVT
Top speed	40.6mph
Av shipping weight	23,408lb
Fuel capacity	132gal

John Deere

Ever green

John Deere dipped a toe in the supertractor market with the 215hp 8010 in 1959. It proved unreliable, but the thoroughly conventional 5010 shown here was a success.

John Deere is the great survivor of the North American tractor industry. It alone managed to survive the hard times of the 1930s and 1980s, and innumerable sticky patches in between, without merger or takeover. Every other famous name in the industry – International, Case, Allis-Chalmers, Oliver and countless others – failed to survive the 20th century independently. John

Deere kept its place at the top of the industry and in 1988, sold over $1 billion worth of machinery.

John Deere's survival technique owed much to Johnny Popper, the well-loved twin-cylinder layout that it stayed loyal to for nearly 50 years. Apparently outdated, the torquey, chuggy Johnny Popper was actually a favourite of American

farmers, and Deere stuck with the layout long after rivals had moved on to four and six-cylinder machines.

The company was not immune to progress though, updating every other aspect of its tractors through the 1930s, '40s and '50s. It was also one of the first US makers to offer a diesel farm tractor. In any case, just as it seemed as if Johnny Popper was terminally outdated, the company swept it aside in favour of a completely new range of four- and six-cylinder tractors, new from stem to stern. Launched to an astonished world in 1960, these formed the basis of a whole new generation of John Deeres.

These weren't the first multi-cylinder tractors the company had ever made and the year before the New Generation was unveiled, John Deere had launched its first supertractor. In fact, it was the first mainstream manufacturer to do so, beating International's big four-wheel drive to market by a year, and the Case Traction King by four years. It wasn't until the early 1970s that every mainstream US tractor manufacturer was offering its own supertractor.

All of which makes the launch of the John Deere 8010 in 1959 sound like a pioneering fairytale. In the event, it was anything but, and although the 8010 was ahead of its time in some ways, there is little doubt that it was launched prematurely.

'With the 10-ton, four-wheel drive 8010, a fleet owner can retire up to three six-plough tractors and their operators; 8010 fuel savings are outstanding too – in recent tests an 8010 with a 31ft tool carrier covered 19 acres an hour at a cost of only 6 cents per acre. Here is truly power for profit.' So proclaimed the original brochure for the 8010, in an attempt to sell the concept of a big supertractor to farmers who had not considered one before. It was certainly big, measuring nearly 20ft in length and tipping the scales at 8.75 tons, and that was without ballast. With 215hp from its Detroit Diesel engine, the 8010 had the sort of power offered only by specialists like Steiger at the time. Not having a suitable power unit itself, John Deere chose Detroit's 6.9-litre six-cylinder two-stroke diesel, driving through a nine-speed synchromesh transmission sourced from a truck.

So big was the 8010 that its maker had to design upsized implements to go with it,

including a 31ft harrow and a 2.5-ton eight-furrow plough. It could pull that big plough at 7mph, a feat which amazed onlookers at the tractor's first demonstration. There were other advanced features too, such as air brakes, two separate hydraulic circuits and a hydraulic clutch with full articulation of 40° each side making the big John Deere surprisingly manoeuvrable.

Unfortunately, once the 8010 began working for customers, the problems began to roll in. The truck transmission in particular proved unable to cope with over 200hp in field work, and failures

Not a supertractor, but with 121hp the John Deere 5010 was one of the most powerful two-wheel-drive rigid tractors of its time.

After the bad experience of the 8010, John Deere played safe and bought-in a Wagner as its next supertractor, but few were sold.

Right: If the 8010 was a false start, the Wagner WA-17 a disappointment, and the 5010 half a class down, then the 7020 was the real thing.

Below: Power for the 7520 came from Deere's 8.7-litre six-cylinder diesel, which was available off the shelf.

Bottom: The 7020/7520 (this is a 175hp 7520) was something of a masterstroke compared with John Deere's earlier supertractors.

Specification

1959 JOHN DEERE 8010

Engine	Detroit Diesel
Engine type	Water-cooled in-line 6, two-stroke
Capacity	6.9 litres
Aspiration	Supercharged
Power @ flywheel	215hp @ 2,100rpm
Power @drawbar	150hp (estimated)
Transmission	9 x 1, constant mesh
Top speed	18.0mph
Av shipping weight	20,700lb

were so frequent that John Deere recalled every single 8010 sold (not that there were many) back to the factory for an upgrade. It fitted a beefier clutch and eight-speed transmission, and made other improvements such as moving the air intake higher up, away from the dust.

They called the result the 8020, sent the upgraded machines back to work and tried to promote the new ones, but the response was disappointing. Despite the success of Steiger, the market for supertractors in the early 1960s was still quite limited, and the failures of the 8010 probably put off a lot of potential buyers. It was also expensive, and despite John Deere's attempt to promote a credit scheme, there were few

takers. When production finally trickled to a stop in 1965, it is thought that fewer than 100 8010s and 8020s had left the factory in total.

The 8010/8020 was a brave project for the company, and was expensive because it used many bought-in or specially made components. John Deere learned these lessons well, and when it began designing an in-house successor, it was determined to make more use of existing, proven components, to cut costs and improve reliability. In the meantime, it needed a supertractor to keep its name in this small but rapidly growing market. After the experience of the 8010, Deere did the sensible thing and brought in a specialist.

Other makers would buy tractors from Steiger and rebadge them, but John Deere chose Wagner, the pioneer which had been building four-wheel-drive articulated tractors since 1953. By 1969, Wagner had a wide range, and John Deere chose the 225hp WA-14 and 280hp WA-17. Both were powered by a 14.1-litre Cummins six-cylinder diesel engine (turbocharged, in the case of the WA-17) and used a 10-speed transmission. In John Deere guise, these were virtually changed, with just the green and yellow colour scheme and appropriate badging.

The agreement signed between John Deere and Wagner on New Year's Eve 1968 allowed for 100 of these hybrids to be produced. In the event, sales were poor, with just 23 WA-14s and 28

WA-17s finding buyers. John Deere dropped the arrangement in 1970, earlier than expected. This did not work out in Wagner's favour, as a clause in the contract prevented them from selling a rival farm tractor for five years after Deere stopped selling the WAs so that effectively put an end to Wagner's farm tractor production.

But if these first two forays into the world of supertractors – the 8010 and the WA – were hardly stunning successes, then the 7020 and 7520 of the early 1970s more than made up for this. They did so by being less expensive, more versatile and easier to use. Unlike the 8010 and

Not as powerful as the Steigers of this world, but at around $13,000 ready to work, the 7520 appealed to a far wider market.

Here's a novel approach to power building! This 7520 has a twin-cylinder 820 John Deere hitched-up tandem style, adding another 70hp or so to the total.

Right: The 7520's two-wheel-drive origins are clearly visible in the slim bonnet line, and by 1975, the tractor needed more power.

Opposite: The great advantage of a big John Deere, as with any supertractor, was in the size of the implement it could pull, thus working much faster than a smaller tractor.

Below: More power, bigger engines (7.6 and 10.0 litres) and the quieter, glassy SoundGard cab marked out the new 30 Series supertractors launched in 1975.

Specification

1971 JOHN DEERE 7020

Engine	John Deere
Engine type	Water-cooled in-line 6
Capacity	6.6 litres
Aspiration	Turbo-intercooled
Power @ PTO	146hp
Power @ flywheel	127hp
Transmission	16 x 4 Synchro Range
Top speed	21.4mph
Operating weight	14,580lb
Min turning radius	17.4ft
Fuel capacity	130gal

The 40 Series had the same massive appearance as its predecessor.

As ever, the engine was John Deere's own, a six-cylinder diesel of 10.1 litres, turbocharged and intercooled, though this one wears a Cummins badge.

WA series, the 7020 launched in 1971 made great use of existing components, especially from the 4020 six-cylinder two-wheel-drive tractor. This cut costs, made servicing easier and brought fewer reliability problems. As John Deere engineer Harold Brock later recalled: 'What we did with the 7020 was to take the 4020 and bisect it and put an engine in the middle. By doing so we took advantage of high-volume production components … and found that we could sell our tractor for $13,000. That put us in

the four-wheel-drive business.' (Quoted in *John Deere New Generation Tractors*, Chester Peterson Jnr and Rod Beemer). The 4020's 6.6-litre six was turbocharged and intercooled to produce 146hp at the PTO, and drove through a 16-speed transmission.

Also, despite its size and pulling power, the 7020 was designed as a smaller, more usable machine than the giant supertractors. It had a wide range of wheel spacings and tyre sizes to suit different crops, had good visibility, and fine ground clearance. It also offered a 1,000rpm PTO – an industry first – and lower link sensing on the three-point hitch. All this made it attractive to smaller row-crop farmers as well as the wheat giants of the Mid West. Demands for more power were partly met with the 7520 of 1972, with a bigger, 8.7-litre engine (another internal off-the-shelf part) offering 175hp. With their usability and keen price, these two tractors were a great success for John Deere, giving it leadership in the four-wheel-drive market, which it never relinquished.

The 7020/7520s were all very well, but they lacked the power of bigger supertractors. Farmers also wanted easier adjustment of the wheel spacings, together with the quiet SoundGard cab which had been an option on smaller two-wheel-drive John Deeres since 1972. All of these concerns were addressed with the updated, upgraded 8430/8630 announced in 1975.

First and most obvious, these tractors had the spacious, glassy Generation II SoundGard cab as standard. This set new standards in comfort,

ergonomics and noise levels, with the bonus of designed-in roll-over protection. This was not just a new cab either, as John Deere like to emphasise that the SoundGard was designed as a unit with the new bodywork, and not simply a separate item bolted on top.

The power question was answered by boring out the existing six-cylinder diesels to 7.6 litres and 10.0 litres, delivering 178hp and 225hp at the PTO respectively. At the engine, that translated into 215hp or 275hp, at 2,100rpm, taking the latest John Deeres up into genuine supertractor territory. Or to put it another way, the 8630 had 20 per cent more torque rise than the 7520. The transmission was still a 16-speed unit, now incorporating a two-speed powershift, but despite the extra power, John Deere was careful to keep the 8000 series abilities as row-crop tractors, thus retaining their all-round appeal. The result was over 3,000 sold in 1975, although to put that in perspective, the company sold over 14,000 examples of its most popular two-wheel-drive tractor, the 4430, that same year.

'More Iron, More Horses', was John Deere's claim for the 40 Series four-wheel drives, which replaced the 30 Series in 1979. On the face of it, these were hardly changed; they looked almost identical to the 30 series, and PTO power was up

only marginally. However, the price had gone up, and a time of high inflation saw the price tag for the 8440 shoot up by $20,000 compared with its 1975 predecessor, to $63,000.

Still, under their skin, there were some improvements. Hitch lift power was up by over 30 per cent, to 8,545lb, and despite the modest power boost, drawbar pull was up substantially as well. The SoundGard cab was even quieter than before (now measured at 80 dB(A)), and in a further nod to the long days drivers were

The SoundGard cab was made quieter for the new series as manufacturers finally took driver welfare seriously.

'More Iron, More Horses', trumpeted the ads, and the 8640 had a few extra; 229hp at the PTO at 2,100rpm.

Get behind one of these on a narrow country road, and you could be in for a long wait; a John Deere 8640 with twin wheels was a big machine.

Accidents will happen, or in the case of this 8440, a partial burn-out. It looks salvageable though.

working, a HydraCushioned seat was added. More tractors were offering in-the-field monitoring systems now, and the 40 Series obliged with the Investigator, which monitored the health of several engine and transmission components. Despite the inflation and uncertain economics of the time, the supertractor market still wanted more power, and in 1982, John Deere delivered.

At the time, the standard route for many supertractor manufacturers was to buy in a

suitable high-horsepower engine from Cummins. For low production volumes, this made economic sense, but John Deere decided to develop its own unit, a V8 diesel which was used by no other green and yellow tractor. This 15.6-litre engine certainly had plenty of power. With turbo and intercooler, it offered 300hp at the PTO, and 370hp at the engine, which finally gave Deere the high-horsepower contender it needed. Turbocharged and intercooled, the new V8 also delivered 270hp at the drawbar, according to tests at the University of Nebraska.

Alongside this new 8850 (recognised by six round headlights, in place of the usual four) were an updated 8450 and 8650. The monitoring system was updated as Investigator II, with a new, faster microprocessor. Both tractors enjoyed a

power boost (up to 290hp for the 8650) with other engine changes to improve efficiency, including a new injection system, new turbocharger and redesigned combustion chamber. Even the cooling fan was redesigned to absorb less power – hard times had persuaded the industry that supertractors had to be efficient as well as powerful. Not for nothing were the 50 Series supertractors advertised as 'Three new ways to tighten your belt.' Mind you, at $118,000 ready to work, the 8850 was an odd way to economise.

If John Deere's very own V8 diesel had acquired any fans, then they would have been

disappointed when the updated 60 series was unveiled in 1988. The V8 was dropped in favour of a bought-in six from Cummins, which despite giving away some capacity to the Deere engine, was slightly more powerful.

Actually, to term the 60 Series as mere 'updates' was to downplay their importance, as these latest supertractors from John Deere were largely new from the ground up. The two 'smaller' 8560 and 8760 still used the familiar 7.6-litre and 10.1-litre six-cylinder diesels, although now with 235hp

Both 40 Series John Deeres (8440 and 8640) shared a higher hitch lift and drawbar pull than the 30s, as well as that quieter cab.

For 1982, the 50 Series brought more efficient six-cylinder diesels, as on this 8450 and an all-new V8 8850.

Specification

1982 JOHN DEERE 8850

Engine	John Deere
Engine type	Water-cooled V8
Capacity	15.6 litres
Aspiration	Turbo-intercooled
Power @ PTO	304hp @ 2,100rpm
Power @ flywheel	270hp
Transmission	16 x 4
Top speed	20.2mph
Av shipping weight	16,520lb
Min turning radius	19ft
Fuel capacity	200gal

The big John Deeres had offered a computerised work monitor since 1979, and this was now updated as Navigator II.

Agricultural John Deeres were always in the familiar green and yellow, while this all-yellow 8650 was probably used in construction.

Specification

1989 JOHN DEERE 8960

Engine	John Deere
Engine type	Water-cooled in-line 6
Capacity	13.9 litres
Aspiration	Turbo-intercooled
Power @ PTO	333hp @ 1,900rpm
Power @ drawbar	308hp
Transmission	12 x 2 (24 x 4 opt)
Top speed	18.6mph
Av shipping weight	35,570lb
Min turning radius	14.5ft
Fuel capacity	183gal

1,900rpm), with 322hp at the PTO and over 300hp available at the drawbar. Actual drawbar pull was slightly less than before, although the new 8960 could handle a hitch lift of almost 14,000lb (up from just over 10,000lb). It was also significantly quieter in the cab – down from 78.0dB(A) to 74.0dB(A).

All the 60 Series supertractors shared a new longer wheelbase chassis, with a greater choice of transmissions than ever before. Standard across the range was a basic 12-speed unit, the Synchro; optional on all three was the 24-speed PowerSync, with partial powershifting. Finally, and offered only on the top two tractors, was the 12-speed full powershift, which allowed clutchless on-the-go shifting across the range. Other new features included a side-access door and a one-piece upper windscreen. With the new 60 Series, it was almost as though John Deere was making a statement. It had suffered serious downsizing and redundancies during the difficult 1980s, but it

The John Deere 8770 was the final update of this venerable supertractor, which had had a major revamp as the 60 Series in 1988.

and 300hp respectively. Replacing that V8 was a 13.9-litre Cummins which was 10 per cent more powerful – engine horsepower was quoted at the same 370hp (although at a lower-rated speed of

Above: All new for 1996, the John Deere 9000 Series replaced the old-generation supertractors, with new engines, new cab and a rubber track option.

Opposite: Perhaps most significant was the new PowerTech engine range, designed and built in-house. This 9400 used a 12.5-litre 425hp version.

had survived independently – the 60 series was a statement of faith in the future.

John Deere had another all-new supertractor on target for the mid-1990s, but in the meantime it needed to update the 8000 series one last time. As a sign of the times, when the 70 Series was launched in 1993, the watchword was 'efficiency'. All tractors were making use of electronics at the time, not just in terms of monitoring work and implements, but in engine control – electronic diesel injection brought increased power and torque along with lower emissions.

To put this in perspective, the 10.1-litre 8870 now offered about the same power as the previous year's range-topping Cummins (or for that matter, Deere's own 15.9-litre V8 a generation earlier), with 300hp at the PTO and 350hp at the engine. Naturally, to avoid embarrassing the top Cummins-powered tractor, this had to be powered-up too, and it was, to 339hp at the PTO, and 400hp at the engine. This 8970 was the most powerful tractor John Deere had ever built, a formidable tool in the field. The mid-range 8770 was unchanged at 256/300hp but the entry-level 8570, still powered by that faithful 7.6-litre six, received a substantial boost, to 205/250hp.

All four 70 Series tractors shared the same transmission options as their predecessors, but a

In the cab, a Field Office option allowed the downloading of a day's work data onto a laptop computer.

The rubber track option, as on this 9300T, was John Deere's response to the Caterpillar Challenger. Fitting twin tracks lost the pivot-steer chassis.

new one was the Field Cruise control. This allowed the driver to set the engine speed below 2,100rpm and maintain a consistent ground speed regardless of varying field conditions. When turning at the headland, they would press an electronic decelerator switch, which would slow the tractor down. The turn completed, the switch was released and the tractor resumed its set speed – cruise control for the prairies.

By 1996 the basic 60 Series design was eight years old, and meanwhile the class standards for power, emissions and electronic controls had all

taken a leap forwards so it was time for a new flagship tractor. The new 9000 Series was launched in 1996 – the '8000' name having been taken by John Deere's top rigid-frame tractor. The 9000 was all-new, but the most obvious change was the replacement of the ageing 7.6 and 10.1-litre power plants, plus the 13.9-litre Cummins, with John Deere's own PowerTech range.

These were state-of-the-art six-cylinder diesels, with electronically controlled unit injectors and turbo-intercooling across the range. The lowest powered was the 8.1-litre unit giving 260hp at the flywheel at a rated 2,100rpm, and fitted to the lead-in 9100 tractor. The mid-range 9200 used a 10.5-litre PowerTech of 310hp while the two top models (9300 and 9400) shared a 12.5-litre version, with 360hp or 425hp. The PowerTechs fulfilled their promises, delivering 8 per cent better fuel efficiency, as well as that extra power.

Transmission choices remained the same as before – 12-speed Synchro, 24-speed PowrSync or 12-speed Power Shift – with top speeds of 17.8–21.3mph. From the driver's point of view, there was much that did change, including the more spacious CommandView cab (carried over from the new 8000 row-crop), and a Field Office option, which allowed the downloading of a day's work data onto a laptop computer.

Another new option was that of rubber tracks, which John Deere now offered on several of its high-horsepower machines – the 9300T and

9400T were a direct response to the success of Caterpillar's rubber-tracked Challenger. The only drawback of course, was that the tracked 9000s could not pivot-steer, making them less manoeuvrable under load than the wheeled versions.

By 2006, the 9000 Series was well into its second update as the 9020. There were five models now, ranging from the 280hp 9120 to the 450hp 9520, the PowerTechs revised with new intake manifold, higher compression and higher camshaft lift. The biggest news was an all-new powershift transmission, which made full use of electronics for ultimate control.

As well as offering more speeds (18 forward, four reverse) this latest option allowed engine and transmission to 'talk' to each other, smoothing out shifts by matching power to suit. The transmission could also select the most efficient ratio for the conditions, by itself, and all the driver had to do was set a few parameters, such as desired throttle position, engine speed and load, and the electronic brain would do the rest.

John Deere supertractors have come a long way since that false start in 1959, recovering from unpromising failure to be the market leader. John Deere the blacksmith, who founded the company back in 1837, would have been proud.

A second update for the 9000 arrived as the 9020 Series, with revised PowerTech engines and all-new powershift transmission.

Despite a legal challenge from Caterpillar over alleged patent infringement, John Deere stuck with its crawler option; this is a 9520T.

Specification

2002 JOHN DEERE 9520

Engine	John Deere PowerTech
Engine type	Water-cooled in-line 6
Capacity	12.5 litres
Aspiration	Turbo-intercooled
Power @ flywheel	425hp @ 2,100rpm
Power @ PTO	302hp
Transmission	12 x 2 (24 x 4 opt)
Top speed	17.8mph
Av shipping weight	33,770lb
Fuel capacity	225gal

Massey Ferguson

The red giants

In the mid-1960s, MF had no high-horsepower two-wheel-drive tractor of its own, let alone a supertractor. This 97 Super was bought in from Minneapolis-Moline.

Long before it was taken over by AGCO, Massey Ferguson was a true multi-national tractor manufacturer. With plants in Britain, France, Canada and the USA, it was one of the few companies that had a genuine understanding of the different requirements of farmers on both sides of the Atlantic. This explains why its supertractor production divides into two distinct groups: the big machines built in the USA, and the smaller, 1200 and 1250 made in Britain, which were a distinctively European take on the whole concept of a pivot-steer four-wheel-drive machine.

This duality is easily explained by Massey Ferguson's origins in the 1953 merger between Canadian controlled Massey Harris, and the

Ferguson company, based in Britain and run by the mercurial Harry Ferguson, but with a factory in Detroit as well as plants in Coventry and France. After the merger, the new Massey Ferguson corporation gradually began to rationalise its two ranges of tractors, with the US and Canadian factories concentrating on larger machines, and those in Britain and France building smaller ones. That made sense, as each was broadly producing what its local market demanded.

Nevertheless, Massey Ferguson was left behind by the early 1960s power race, and had to buy in the 75hp Minneapolis-Moline Gvi, badging and selling it as the 95 Super. The company's own high-horsepower tractors arrived later in the decade, notably the 90hp 1100 and 120hp 1130, both powered by a Perkins six-cylinder diesel. These were joined in 1968 by the 1150, using a 135hp Perkins V8.

These were all two-wheel-drive tractors, and it wasn't until 1971 that Massey Ferguson finally launched its first supertractor. Rather than buy in someone else's design, the company developed its own, and built it in Toronto, Canada. The MF 1500 was a conventional pivot-steer machine, with four-wheel drive by equal-sized wheels. The engine was slightly unusual, in that it was a Caterpillar 3150 V8 with the exceptionally high-rated speed of 3,000rpm, making it higher revving than any other supertractor. This 9.4-litre unit drove through a 12-speed transmission over a range of 2.3–21.3mph. According to tests at the University of Nebraska, it produced 152hp at the drawbar at that sky-high rated speed.

Alongside the 1500 was the 1800; very similar in most respects except for the 10.5 litre Caterpillar 3160 V8, which produced 178hp at the drawbar, and still rated at a relatively high, 2,800rpm. Even this engine was related to that of the 1500, with the same 4.5in bore but with an extra half-inch on the stroke. This too used a 12-speed transmission, with the slightly lower rated speed giving 2.1–19.8mph. According to the university's results (both tractors were submitted for test in 1971) the 1800 was also slightly more efficient than its smaller brother, delivering 13.49hp hr/gallon against 12.49hp hr/gallon.

Although designed primarily for Stateside conditions, the 1500 and 1800 also achieved some success in the UK and mainland Europe.

This was partly due to the simple economics of running a big tractor, which given sufficient space, can usually work faster and more efficiently than a small one.

Another factor was brand loyalty. In Britain, very few people had heard of Steiger or Versatile, and even John Deere was fairly rare at that time. Every farmer in the land knew Massey Ferguson of course and its familiar red colour scheme – most of them owned a two-wheel-drive MF or a 'little grey Fergie' as well. For them, if they were going to buy a big supertractor, then the MF 1500 or 1800 was the obvious choice.

As powerful as they were, the big MFs were nothing to write home about in a class where

A sad end for this 97. The main purpose of the model was to act as a stopgap until Massey Ferguson had a high-horsepower contender of its own.

Massey Ferguson was a good customer of Perkins which built V8 diesel engines. The result was a whole line of V8 MFs, two-wheel-drive hot rods that were soon overtaken by the four-wheel-drive tide.

Specification

1971 MASSEY FERGUSON 1800

Engine	Caterpillar 3160
Engine type	Water-cooled V8
Capacity	10.5 litres
Power @ drawbar	178hp
Transmission	12 x 4
Top speed	19.8mph
Av shipping weight	16,750lb
Min turning radius	17ft
Fuel capacity	100gal

There's something special about this beautifully restored V8-powered 2775 from the early 1970s.

Massey Ferguson's six-cylinder 1135 and V8 1150 of the late 1960s were soon joined by the company's first supertractor.

200+hp was increasingly common. So, in 1975, they received an upgrade as the 1505 and 1805. Power still came from a Caterpillar V8, although now it was the 10.4-litre 3208, which in the 1505, offered 174hp at the PTO, or 185hp at the flywheel. In the 1805, this was uprated to 192hp and 210hp, both models rated at 2,800rpm, giving a top speed of 19.8mph through the same 12 forward and four reverse transmission as before. There were other changes, including a fully independent

1,000rpm PTO and the choice of a Category II or III three-point linkage.

All of these, from 1500 to 1805, were medium-weight supertractors rather than true heavyweights, the average shipping weight of the 1500 for example, was 7.36 tons. They could articulate 40° in either direction and had 15° of oscillation, the latter to keep all four wheels in contact with the ground. Careful design ensured that weight distribution was 60 per cent front, 40 per cent rear, with a perfect 50/50 when an implement was hooked up. Many owners fitted dual wheels, in which case ground pressure of

around 8psi could be expected, and wheel slip of less than 10 per cent.

The Massey Ferguson 1500 and 1800 were traditional supertractors, born of North American conditions and aimed squarely at US and Canadian farmers, but the 1200, which appeared the following year, could not have been more different. True, it was a four-wheel-drive machine with equal-sized wheels and pivot-steer chassis, but there (unless you count the Massey Ferguson badges), the resemblance ended.

It was said to be the success of the 1500/1800 in 1971 that persuaded MF management to launch a British equivalent. If true, then the corporation's British arm wasted no time, as the new MF 1200 was launched the following year. It had a huge impact, for the simple reason that very few farmers in Britain or mainland Europe had seen a four-wheel-drive supertractor in the metal before. Many had seen pictures of Steigers and Versatiles in the farming press, but here was a tractor on show at your local Massey Ferguson dealer (and there were plenty of those in Britain), at a relatively affordable price. Until then, the only four-wheel drive tractors (apart from the low production Doe Triple-D) were conversions of conventional skid units, such as the Roadless and County.

The MF 1200 was different from any of those, although it did use a familiar Perkins diesel, the 6.354 5.8-litre six which had powered the earlier 1100 and 1130. In the 1200, there was no turbocharger, and power figures amounted to 105hp at 2,400rpm, or 91hp at the PTO. These set no records, and made the 1200 less powerful than many two-wheel-drive tractors already being turned out of Massey Ferguson factories.

The 1200's secret lay in its equal-sized wheels and perfect 50/50 weight distribution when an

The little 1200 proved highly successful in practice, thanks to its fine traction and good manoeuvrability.

A graphic example of just how tight the 1200 could turn, combining a high work rate with the ability to make the best of small and awkward spaces.

Right: The 1200 used a conventional pivot-steer system. In effect, it was a full-size supertractor, but scaled down.

Far right: A standard three-point hitch meant the 1200/1250 could hook up to any existing implement.

Below: The narrow dimensions of the 1200 are clear in this picture, these being perfect for English country lanes.

Far left: Power came from the well-proven Perkins 5.8-litre diesel; 105hp does not sound much perhaps, but it still did a useful job.

Left: The dashboard looks basic by 21st century standards, but this was really all that drivers expected in 1971.

Below: A well-kept Massey Ferguson 1250, which represented the only major update of the 1200.

Specification

1972 MASSEY FERGUSON 1200

Engine	Perkins 6.354
Engine type	Water-cooled in-line 6
Capacity	5.8 litres
Power @ flywheel	105hp @ 2,400rpm
Power @ PTO	91hp
Transmission	12 x 4
Top speed	17.5mph
Operating weight	13,676lb
Min turning radius	12ft
Fuel capacity	70gal

Massey Ferguson replaced the Canadian-built 1505/1805 with the bigger 4000 series in late 1978, with a choice of the 225hp 4800 or the 265hp 4840, as shown here.

All 4000 series MFs used the same 18-speed partial powershift transmission, the big cab being another common factor.

implement was attached. This gave impressive traction, especially in difficult conditions, and demonstrations soon won over the sceptics. Not only that, but the 1200 combined 40° pivot steering with a relatively small size, so it was remarkably manoeuvrable as well, with a turning radius of just 12ft. A top speed of 17.5mph made it usable for road haulage as well, and one UK-based 1200 was even converted into a road-based truck recovery vehicle! Bigger farmers in Britain and the rest of Europe could not fail to see the advantages, and the 1200 sold well.

So successful was the 1200 that it was seven years before it was upgraded, as the 1250. There was only a small power increase from the venerable Perkins, to 112hp at 2,400rpm, with 96hp at the PTO, but by now MF's baby supertractor had long since been overtaken in the power race. Its strength lay, not in ultimate power, but in its combination of superb traction and manoeuvrability in tricky conditions. The 1250 also added a heavier-duty drive shaft, stronger three-point hitch, higher capacity hydraulics and new rear-axle epicyclic drives.

However, time was catching up, and the 1250 lasted only three years, with production ending in 1982, but the series remains something of a landmark. It was the only pivot-steer supertractor built in Britain, was arguably one of the few designed for European conditions, and introduced many Continental farmers to the advantages of this layout.

With the 1200/1500 and 1500/1800, Massey Ferguson had covered the light and medium-weight supertractor sectors very well. Yet they still lacked a true heavyweight, one that could battle not just with specialists like Steiger, but with the mainstream US tractor manufacturers which were also building their own giants for the prairies.

When the MF 4000 series was launched in 1978, it effectively replaced the 1505/1805, but was really a class higher. There were four models: the 4800 and 4840 launched in the autumn of 1978; the 4880 in November '79; and the high-power 4900 a few months later, in the spring of 1980. All were based on the same big-scale

dimensions: a 21ft overall length enclosing an 11ft 5in wheelbase with a width of 9ft.

Massey Ferguson had chosen Caterpillar as engine supplier for its first supertractor, but now it followed just about everyone else and turned to Cummins instead. All four 4000 series tractors employed the same basic Cummins V8 of 14.8 litres, naturally aspirated for the 4800 (225hp) and 4840 (265hp), and with a turbo on the 4880 (320hp) and 4900 (375hp). This finally took MF into the hyper-horsepower sector, and in fact, the 4900 was one of the most powerful tractors available during the 1980s.

Whichever 4000 series you chose, the transmission was an 18-speed unit, incorporating a three-speed powershift delivering a top speed of 19.2mph. They were also notable for a particularly roomy cab offering excellent visibility, and for their electronic three-point hitch. The latter was a first on the American market, underlining Massey Ferguson's lead in developing tractor electronics. In the case of the hitch, this allowed more precise implement control, even in varying field conditions. The whole 4000 series was dropped in 1986.

The final chapter in the Massey supertractor story was the 5200 series, offered between 1989 and 1991, but if truth be told, it was actually built by someone else. The 5200 was a major upgrade of the 4000, though rather than undertake the job itself, MF handed the whole project over to a specialist. A deal was struck with McConnell Tractors of Kinston, North Carolina.

Specification

1989 MASSEY FERGUSON 5200

Engine	(1) Cummins NTA855
	(2) Detroit Diesel Series 60
Engine type	Water-cooled in-line 6
Capacity (1)	14.0 litres
	(2) 12.7 litres
Aspiration	Turbo-intercooled
Power @ flywheel (1)	375hp @ 2,100rpm
	(2) 390hp @ 2,100prm
Transmission	12-speed manual (full powershift option)
Top speed	17.6mph
Av shipping weight	36,000lb
Min turning radius	14.5ft
Fuel capacity	158gal

J. Ward McConnell bought the four-wheel-drive tractor arm of the Massey Combine Corporation, and undertook to produce a new supertractor based on an updated 4000 series, which he would then sell to MF exclusively. There would be two models of 300–400hp sold with MF badges through MF dealers.

The 5200 series was the result, and it looked quite different from the 4000. That was because McConnell designed new bodywork and cab to

Specification

1980 MASSEY FERGUSON 4900

Engine	Cummins VT-903
Engine type	Water-cooled V8
Capacity	14.8 litres
Aspiration	Turbo
Power @ flywheel	375hp @ 2,600rpm
Power @ PTO	320hp
Transmission	18-speed, partial powershift
Top speed	19.2mph
Av shipping weight	27,000lb
Min turning radius	17ft
Fuel capacity	158gal

Higher-powered 4000s like this 4880 arrived in late 1979 and early 1980, although all used the same Cummins V8 engine.

Above: The complete line-up of MF 4000 series supertractors, before they were sold to McConnell Manufacturing.

Opposite: Now part of AGCO, Massey Ferguson is not required to build a supertractor any more, concentrating on small/medium two- and four-wheel-drive machines.

underline the new regime, but the 5200 was also re-engined. Cummins still provided one of the power options, a 14.0-litre straight-six, offering 375hp at 2,100rpm. If that wasn't enough, the alternative was a Detroit Diesel Series 60, a four-stroke 12.7-litre engine of 390hp. The company claimed this engine had been tested for 20,000 hours doing agricultural work, while the familiar Cummins had completed over 20 million hours in the field. Both engines were turbo-intercooled, and had the option of 12-speed manual or 12-speed powershift transmissions. Whichever combination one chose, the 5200 had a turning radius of 14.6ft, quite an achievement for a full-size supertractor.

The arrangement between MF and McConnell lasted less than three years and in 1991, McConnell began selling the tractors under its own name and in bright yellow livery. Detroit Diesel's Series 60 was now the only power unit offered, with 320hp in the Marc 900 tractor, or 425hp in the Marc 1000. These were produced until 1994, when AGCO took over McConnell, and the yellow Marc tractors were transformed into silver AGCOSTARS. By then, AGCO had also swallowed up Massey Ferguson, but wanted the brand to concentrate on its core strength of small and medium-sized machines. AGCOSTAR would be the new brand of supertractor sold by the AGCO corporation, and this marked the end of the MF supertractor story.

Minneapolis-Moline/Oliver

Rearguard action

The Minneapolis-Moline G1000 Vista, typical of the big, two-wheel-drive machines offered by the company.

By the late 1960s, many of North America's smaller tractor makers had either merged, or disappeared altogether. Minneapolis-Moline and Oliver came into the former category, both having been taken over by the White Corporation in the early 1960s. They were long-established names in American farming and both had been formed by mergers of their own back in

1929 and had a good record in tractor innovation.

Oliver had been offering a high-compression six-cylinder engine in the 1930s, when most rivals stuck with two cylinders or four. Minneapolis-Moline meanwhile, could boast of a whole series of industry firsts, including four valves per cylinder, a five-speed transmission, a

Minneapolis-Moline and Oliver both had experience of high-horsepower two-wheel tractors. This is an Oliver Super 99.

Oliver's Super 99 was also offered with a supercharged GM two-stroke diesel engine, giving 72hp at a wailing 1,675rpm.

Minneapolis-Moline specialised in large, rigid chassis tractors through the 1960s, such as this special for rice cultivation.

The 169hp A4T-1600 soon followed the 139hp A4T-1400. Like the original, it made extensive use of existing parts to cut production costs.

well-equipped cab and a genuine high-speed tractor, the latter two featuring in the 40mph UDLX 'Comfortractor' of 1938. MM was also an early proponent of smaller (sub-100hp) four-wheel-drive tractors, notably with the M504 in 1962.

By the late 1960s, these two erstwhile rivals were increasingly sharing components, as parent company White tried to turn a profit out of its new farm equipment interests. The A4T supertractor was their last gasp, produced in the last couple of years before White dropped the

old brand names, and launched its own range of supertractors under the White Field Boss name.

Despite this, the A4T was a genuine Minneapolis-Moline design, using largely MM parts, though it was built in a White factory. Through the 1960s, the company had been concentrating on its bigger tractors, as White's Cockshutt and Oliver subsidiaries had the smaller models covered already. But with its established expertise in four-wheel drive, MM was the obvious choice to design a pivot-steer supertractor for the parent company, to take advantage of this growing market.

A Minneapolis-Moline dealer in Arkansas had actually built his own four-wheel-drive pivot-steer machine back in 1958, using MM components, and the company president visited him to examine the tractor before making the decision to back a factory-built version. From the start, the new tractor would have to use as many off-the-shelf parts as possible in order to keep costs to a minimum. Design work began in March 1969, and use of some existing parts meant that a running prototype was working just two months later. By November, the A4T was ready to start production.

It was the use of existing parts that resulted in this impressively fast translation from

Specification

1969 MINNEAPOLIS-MOLINE A4T-1600

Engine	Minneapolis-Moline D585
Engine type	Water-cooled in-line 6
Capacity	9.6 litres
Power @ flywheel	169hp @ 2,200rpm
Power @ PTO	143hp
Transmission	10 x 2 manual
Top speed	22.2mph
Operating weight	19,850lb

drawing board to ready-to-work tractor. The A4T's power unit was MM's own D504A-6 six-cylinder diesel, with 139hp, while the five-speed transmission came out of the G1350 two-wheel-drive tractor, with a two-speed transfer case added to give ten speeds in all. The brakes came from the G1350 as well, and the drive axles from the G950. Hydraulics were also plucked from the corporate parts bin, along with wheels, radiators, hubs, instrumentation and seat.

Nevertheless, some major parts did have to be designed and built from scratch, including the front and rear frames, an articulation joint, driveline system, the cab, bodywork, fuel tanks and wiring. The original A4T-1400 was soon joined by the LPG-powered A4T-1600. Minneapolis-Moline had long been a champion of LPG, a less efficient but cheaper fuel than diesel, and the A4T was the only supertractor to ever offer such an option. Alongside the gas tractor was a diesel 1600, this one using the company's existing D585 six, borrowed from the G1350 which offered 169hp at 2,200rpm, enabling the A4T to rumble along the road at up to 22.2mph. Not surprisingly, the diesel 1600 was the biggest seller of the three, with over 600 built in 1971.

However, not all of these were sold as Minneapolis-Molines. Brand loyalty was still a strong factor in the tractor buying decision at the time, and White had several brands to look after. So it made sense to sell the A4T under various guises. To keep Oliver dealers happy, it was painted green and sold as the Oliver 2455 and

2655, with 244 of the latter being sold. Meanwhile, White wanted to establish its own name in the tractor market, so marketed the A4T as the White Plainsman as well, although only in Canada.

This badge engineering did not last long, and when White launched the new Field Boss range in 1974, they were sold as Whites only, not as Minneapolis-Moline or Oliver. The colour schemes of yellow and white (MM) and green (Oliver) did return briefly on the 1989 two-wheel-drive White American range, but in truth, the last Minneapolis-Moline machine was the A4T supertractor.

The MM supertractor only lasted in production for three years, but gave the parent company a toehold before the new generation of White Field Boss tractors was ready.

Confused identity? The A4T-1400 nearer the camera also wears a White badge while the A4T-1600 behind it has the original MM badge.

Steiger
Bigger by design

The Steiger brothers had no great ambitions to become tractor manufacturers, but that's what they did. This early Series II Steiger Cougar is in the distinctive lime-green livery that marked out all Steigers until the takeover by Case.

One name above all others is associated with the four-wheel-drive articulated supertractor: Steiger. The big lime-green machines have come to represent the epitome of the breed. As Ferrari is to cars and Harley-Davidson is to motorcycles, so Steiger is to monster tractors. Yet Doug and Maurice Steiger were not pioneers. They did not – as is often thought – invent the four-wheel-drive pivot-steer layout. When they finally went into full production in 1961, Wagner had been

producing similar machines for seven years, and John Deere had launched its short-lived 8010 in 1959.

Pioneers they might not be, but there is no denying that Steiger tractors still have an imposing presence. That is at least down partly to the brothers' fondness for naming their vehicles after big cats – Cougar, Lion, Panther and Puma – suggesting a combination of power, strength and grace. Not only that, but Steigers have

proved to be tough, reliable and long-lived machines. On the wheat prairies of America's Mid West, they could clock up 15,000 or 20,000 hours or more, and still be running as well as the day they left the factory. The big green tractors also proved easy to maintain, using off-the-shelf components rather than specialised parts. So, although Steiger wasn't a pioneer, and was later swallowed up by Case, it stands out as a supertractor success story.

Starting a new tractor dynasty was probably the last thing on Doug and Maurice Steigers' minds when they began building their first tractor in the winter of 1957/58. Aided by their father John, they were dairy farmers at Red Lake Falls, Minnesota, and became frustrated at the lack of a suitable high-horsepower tractor, which they were convinced could work faster than a conventional machine. At that time, the most powerful tractor offered by the likes of Case, John Deere and

Steiger never built its own engines, buying in proprietary units such as this Caterpillar V8.

Allis-Chalmers was around 60hp with two-wheel drive. The brothers reasoned that a more powerful machine, with four-wheel drive to transmit a greater number of horses, could work faster and more efficiently than any of those.

Four circular headlights denote the Series III Steigers, built between 1976 and 1983; the most popular line of all.

A Steiger Panther ST310 with the Steigermatic option, which added a torque converter to the Allison ten-speed transmission.

A Cougar ST270. Steiger named nearly all its tractors after big cats – far more evocative than the usual string of numbers.

The tractor they built during those winter months was something of a hybrid, consisting of parts that were easily available or just lying around the farm. Some bits came from a Euclid earth mover, others from trucks. Even the famous lime-green colour scheme was inherited from quarry machinery – a local mining company had ordered the paint for its new fleet, but was unhappy with the shade. The Steigers got wind of this and offered to buy the whole batch. For

Specification

1963 STEIGER 1250

Engine	Detroit Diesel 4-53N
Engine type	Water-cooled in-line 4
Capacity	3.5 litres
Power @ flywheel	130hp @ 2,300rpm
Transmission	12-speed manual
Top speed	17mph
Av shipping weight	13,800lb
Fuel capacity	90gal (US)

nearly 30 years, lime green would be the colour of Steiger.

Power came from a 238hp six-cylinder Detroit diesel, and Steiger No. 1, as it has been retrospectively named, was, 'a numb lump', according to tractor author Peter Simpson. It weighed 15,000lb (monstrous for the time) and had ponderous tiller steering. Built in a barn, it was promptly nicknamed 'Barney'.

Barney the home-built special, could work harder and faster than any other tractor. It was reliable too, and would notch up over 10,000 hours work in the field before being pensioned off.

In a way, what the brothers had done was no more than a little lateral thinking. A whole raft of high-horsepower components – engines, transmissions and axles – were already in use and well proven in quarries, in road construction equipment and big trucks. This included engines from Detroit Diesel, CAT or Cummins, axles from Clarke, and transmissions from Allison. Applying this know-how to agricultural tractors was, with hindsight, simply a logical step.

Naturally, when neighbouring farmers saw how well the new tractor was performing in the fields, they began to ask for replicas. They weren't that keen on the tiller steering, but they certainly liked the look of the work rates. The Steigers did not rush into mass production however, and in fact, it was not until 1961 that the first production tractor was launched. The 1200 was smaller than that big 'numb lump', with a conventional steering wheel in place of the tiller, and a slightly more modest 118hp Detroit Diesel, although it still had an operating weight of 8 tons.

Only three of these 1200s were actually built on the Red Lakes Fall farm, and with most work done by the Steigers themselves, but its reception confirmed that the market was ready for an affordable four-wheel-drive high-horsepower tractor. Things moved up a gear in 1963, when a range of three machines was launched: the 1250, 1700 and 2200. All were Detroit Diesel powered, ranging from 130hp to 238hp, mated to a 12-speed transmission in the case of the smallest 1250, and a nine-speed shared by its two big

One feature of the Series III Steigers was the Safari cab which was spacious, glassy and complete with air conditioning.

A later Series II Cougar from 1980–81. The 'PTA' referred to the narrow chassis option with automatic transmission.

What better way to promote a monster American circus than with a monster American tractor?

By the late 1970s/1980s, Steiger was facing plenty of competition, such as from Ford's 946 (seen in the background) but it was still the leading supertractor manufacturer.

Specification

1969 STEIGER TIGER SERIES 1

Engine	Cummins
Engine type	Water-cooled V8
Capacity	14.8 litres
Aspiration	Turbo
Power @ flywheel	320hp @ 2,600rpm
Transmission	10-speed manual
Top speed	17.7mph
Av shipping weight	21,000lb

brothers. Meanwhile, Doug and Maurice were joined by salesman Earl Christianson, who had been wondering why the high-horsepower technology of road construction work couldn't be applied to tractors. At Steiger, he met men of like mind, and his work would contribute greatly to the company's rapid growth.

The three existing tractors were joined by a bigger, 3300 powered by a V8 Detroit Diesel of 318hp. It tipped the scales at nearly 14 tons, yet could reach a sprightly 22.7mph. Just in case anyone hadn't got the message, all V8-powered Steigers had a massive 'V' cut into their front

end, which consisted of ⅜in thick steel. Another 300hp Steiger, the 800 Tiger, joined the range too, the first to be powered by a Cummins engine.

This was all very well, but demand was beginning to outstrip the Steigers' ability to supply. Tractors were still being built in the barn (they are still officially known as the 'Barn series') and although the payroll had swollen to 20 men, the Steiger brothers were doing much of the work themselves. Despite the efforts of Earl Christianson, the tiny company still didn't have the resources to promote its tractors nation wide.

In 1969, a solution appeared in the form of a business consortium, which brought in a chunk of cash, enabling Steiger to move into a disused tank factory in Fargo, North Dakota. They had built 126 tractors on the farm, but now it was time to move on.

To underline this new era a new line of tractors was launched. These were the Series I, perhaps most notable for bringing in the big cat names across the range, which would be a feature of Steiger machines for nearly 20 years. They were also far more sophisticated than the early Barn series, with a 'Climatized Cab'. Mounted separately from the chassis, this was pressurised to keep out dust, and was equipped with both heating and air conditioning.

The first Series I Steigers to emerge from the new factory were the 175hp Wildcat and 200hp Super Wildcat, both powered by CAT V8s, together with the 310hp Tiger, which had a 14.8-litre Cummins V8. The following year, they were joined by the Bearcat (225hp CAT V8), then the Cougar (300hp CAT straight-six) and in 1973, the most powerful Steiger yet, the 320hp Turbo

Tiger, using a turbocharged version of that big Cummins. All drove though a ten-speed transmission, either a Fuller or a Dana Spicer unit. It was a big range, although this was something that typified Steiger, offering a complete range of supertractors where most rivals had only one or two on offer.

By now, the company was selling through over 60 dealers across North America, finding that it wasn't just Minnesotan dairy farmers who appreciated the benefits of big power. Vegetable farmers in California, rice growers in the South and wheat men in Washington all joined the ranks of Steiger owner/operators. One in three buyers of machines like this were opting for a Steiger, which, when you consider that the mainstream manufacturers were starting to wake up to this market, was quite an achievement.

The tractors were updated as Series IIs in 1974, which saw the dropping of the 'smallest' (a relative term) Wildcat, and the debut of a new

Specification

1975 STEIGER PANTHER II

Engine	Cummins NT-855
Engine type	Water-cooled in-line 6
Capacity	14.1 litres
Power @ PTO	310hp @ 2,100rpm
Power @ drawbar	250hp (est.)
Transmission	10-speed manual

Panther (straight-six Cummins powered). Also new was the option of adjustable row-crop axles on the Super Wildcat and Bearcat, which offered a choice of widths between 60in and 90in. Spotting these row-crop Steigers is easy, as the model number was prefixed by 'RC', while fixed-axle machines became 'STs'.

Meanwhile, demand for the market-leading supertractor continued to grow. In the mid-

This Cougar ST280 and Panther ST325 both have the standard Steiger chassis, denoted by 'ST' prefix in their designations. The ST325 was a popular model and a few were sold as 'RC' row-crop tractors, with adjustable axle widths.

1970s, Steiger began to export widely for the first time, and this market promised to be even bigger than the domestic one – one estimate put it at four times the size. Not all of these supertractors went to wide open spaces, as despite being designed with the big acreages of Missouri and Dakota in mind, the lower powered models at least, proved adaptable to larger farms and contractors in the UK and mainland Europe. Their secret of course (shared with other articulated 4x4s) was that the hinged chassis made them as manoeuvrable as a much smaller, rigid-chassis, two-wheel-drive machine.

In fact, Steiger was doing so well that only five years after moving to Fargo, it had outgrown its new factory. In 1974, work was started on a new, much bigger plant of 420,000sq ft. Less than a year later, it was up and running, employing 1,100 people and able to produce supertractors at the astonishing rate of one every 18 minutes.

Meanwhile, Steiger was working on a new generation of tractors, although it also liked to keep the competition guessing. For instance, it actually built a giant, two-wheel-drive rigid-chassis tractor, badged up in authentic Steiger green, to fool industry spies into thinking that the Fargo factory was developing a smaller machine. It wasn't of course, and the two-wheel-drive Steiger was soon scrapped.

A more serious project was the Triple Steiger, a response to the search for ever more horsepower. Big Bud had overtaken Steiger, offering the most powerful production supertractor ever built, and this was Fargo's answer. Three Cougar engines were mounted in an articulated chassis to deliver a combined 750hp, but this super-powered prototype failed to live up to its promise – one bystander describing it as 'terrible', and the project was dropped. A similar fate befell TST650, a 1976 project to join two Panthers into a 650hp machine.

The fact was, Steiger did not need to become involved with such radical alternatives. For one thing, the company was developing a lucrative sideline in making tractors for other concerns. It wasn't yet worth mainstream manufacturers building their own supertractors, but they were happy to buy machines in from Steiger, painted and badged as their own. In the early 1970s, some Steigers sold in Canada came in the orange livery of Canadian Co-op Implements, while the

Allis-Chalmers 440, offered between 1972 and 1975, was a Steiger sold through A-C dealers in the USA. Also, Ford's long-running FW series, which appeared in various guises from 1977 until 1985, was simply a Steiger, repainted and rebadged to suit. International beat a path to Steiger's door too, but designed the 66 and 86 Series itself, using many of its own components, simply contracting Steiger to build them.

Meanwhile, Steiger wasn't neglecting its own lime-green range, and in 1976 these were updated as the Series III. These were introduced to dealers in Florida, and in a piece of pure circus showmanship, a 'lion tamer' cracked his whip as the new Panthers and Bearcats roared into the ring.

As ever, it was the sheer choice offered that marked Steiger out from every other supertractor manufacturer – take all the engine and axle

Opposite: A 1978 Panther ST310, this one with a 13.9-litre six-cylinder Cummins engine.

Above: The Series IV Steigers appeared in 1983, ranging from the 225hp Bearcat to the 360hp Panther. The 525hp Tiger IV joined the line-up the following year.

Below: A Series IV Panther 1360. Once more, there was a huge range of tractors to choose from and now including a Komatsu engine option.

Battered it might be, but this Series IV Panther still looks like it's capable of hard work. The KP badge indicates Cummins power with six-speed powershift transmission.

The 1986 Puma 1000 was a radical departure for Steiger; smaller than its predecessors, and with a steerable front axle to improve manoeuvrability.

options into account, and there were 15 separate Series IIIs available, ranging from the 210hp Wildcat to the 470hp Tiger. These boiled down to just four basic models however – the Wildcat III, Bearcat III, Cougar III and Panther III – with the Tiger III added the following year. Apart

from the Wildcat, they all came with a choice of CAT or Cummins power, with six-cylinders only for the Bearcat and Cougar, a choice of V8 or six on the Panther and Tiger, and CAT V8 only for the Wildcat.

All had ten-speed constant-mesh transmissions (automatic was still a few years away) and all shared the new Safari cab. This was more spacious than ever before, with better visibility and more conveniently positioned controls, and of course, it was air conditioned. Only the Wildcat had the option of row-crop adjustable axles, still offering widths of 60–90 inches, and making the tractor able to cope with a whole variety of different crops, such as sunflower and maize. Smaller farmers, looking to trade up to their first supertractor, were likely to go for this option.

As well as the row-crop Wildcat, the Bearcat, Cougar and Panther also had the option of a narrow frame from 1977. It came with another innovation, an electronic PTO, which was a first for an articulated supertractor. Limited to 125hp, the PTO was hydrostatic and featured constant rpm so it would not slow if the engine did. All Steigers so fitted had the 'PT' designation. With their narrow frame, the PT tractors were particularly manoeuvrable for such large

machines, and the Bearcat PT could turn as tightly as a 100hp two-wheel-drive tractor. A three-point linkage was another option, making this supertractor more adaptable than ever.

This sophistication was all very well, but Steiger's main selling point was still power, and plenty of it. That was the thinking behind the new Tiger III, also launched in 1977. At 450hp, this wasn't the most powerful tractor on the market (this was the 525hp Big Bud), but the

Tiger came a good second. Power came from a Caterpillar V8 of 18.1 litres, producing its 450hp at 2,200rpm. This was later joined by an optional Cummins six, of 18.9 litres and 470hp. In both cases the power unit was too much for the standard Spicer ten-speed transmission, so they were provided with an Allison powershift, with six forward speeds and one reverse.

The Tiger III was Steiger's most powerful tractor yet and the biggest too, at 191in wide by 289in long. It weighed over 45,000lb (more than 20 tons) and carried 385 US gallons of diesel fuel, yet it was relatively fuel-efficient and had a turning radius of just 18ft.

Manual transmissions were rapidly being overtaken by powershifts, even among smaller two-wheel-drive tractors, and Steiger responded with an automatic option in 1980. 'Steigermatic' was actually an Allison ten-speed unit with a two-speed transfer case and a torque converter. It could be locked into each gear to increase efficiency, but otherwise brought a new ease of operation for Steiger drivers. Tractors with this option were 'PTAs', having an electronic PTO as part of the package.

By this time, it looked as if Steiger could do little wrong. It was the acknowledged

Case or Steiger? After the 1986 takeover, the tractors were sold in red and black Case-IH colours, but were still built by Steiger.

Specification

1977 STEIGER COUGAR III

Engine	Cummins NT-855*
Engine type	Water-cooled in-line 6
Capacity	14.1 litres
Aspiration	Turbo
Power @ flywheel	280hp @ 2,200rpm
Power @ drawbar	210hp
Transmission	10-speed manual
Top speed	16.7mph
Operating weight	29,800lb

Various engine options available

Above: The big cats became the Case 9000 series, although a Steiger grille badge was added later, to make the heritage clear.

Right: The only crawler ever built in Steiger's factory, the Case/Steiger four-track Quadtrac.

supertractor specialist, which had kept its products up to date and exported them all over the world. By the end of the 1970s, 10,000 Steigers had been built, then, in 1982, it diversified, introducing an industrial range of yellow-painted supertractors aimed at the construction and mining sectors.

Unfortunately, the 1980s saw a slump in farming worldwide, especially in the USA. For the first time in a long while, farmers began to cut back on capital expenditure, with the purchase of expensive supertractors being the first thing to go. For Steiger, this signalled the end of the boom years and the beginning of a

Specification

1986 STEIGER BEARCAT 1000

Engine	Caterpillar 3306B
Engine type	Water-cooled in-line 6
Capacity	10.5 litres
Aspiration	Turbo
Power @ flywheel	235hp @ 2,100rpm
Power @ PTO	218hp
Transmission	12-speed full powershift
Top speed	17.3mph
Av shipping weight	28,575lb

Above: The Quadtrac was aimed to meet the Caterpillar Challenger head on, and made a more efficient use of power on turns.

Below: Tracks apart, the Quadtrac was mechanically similar to the wheeled 9000 series. This is a 9380.

Opposite: An imposing frontage for Quadtrac, which clearly shows the big footprint offered by those rubber tracks.

difficult decade that would result in bankruptcy.

No-one could accuse the company of resting on its laurels however. In 1983, both the updated Series IV Steigers and the new 1000 were launched. It was business as usual for the Series IVs, spanning from the 225hp Bearcat up to the 360hp Panther, which were joined in 1984 by a 525hp Cummins 18.9-litre turbo-intercooled six, in the Tiger IV. For the first time, Steiger strayed from the Cummins/CAT duo, offering a 325hp Komatsu unit in the Panther.

Transmissions available were the now-familiar Steigermatic, a 20-speed manual or in the Tiger, the Allison six-speed powershift. The Series IVs remained in production right up to 1988 and alongside these updated originals was the new Panther 1000. Although a new design, this

followed the familiar Steiger layout, with the option of Cummins or CAT power, in 325hp, 335hp or 400hp forms. New features were a redesigned Safari cab with a sloping nose for improved visibility and a 12-speed powershift transmission. More radical was the Puma 1000, unveiled in 1986. Intended to compete with big, two-wheel-drive tractors, this 'baby' Steiger had adjustable row-crop axles (60–130 inches) and innovatively, featured a steerable front axle as well as the usual articulated chassis. This made it one of the most manoeuvrable supertractors ever, a true alternative to a big two-wheel-drive John Deere or a Case-IH. Power came from a 190hp Case six mated to a 12-speed powershift.

Other 1000 series Steigers joined the range, but the company could not escape the general slump in tractor sales. In an effort to cut costs, it began to share components between tractors (Bearcat and Cougar now having a common chassis for example), but with the big factory producing at just 25 per cent capacity, the end was near. This came in 1986 when the company posted larger than expected losses. It filed for Chapter 11 bankruptcy, and that was the end of Steiger as an independent company, but not the end of the Steiger name.

Despite the slump, the company's supertractor expertise and production facilities would be a prize for any mainstream manufacturer, and before the year was out, the Fargo factory had been bought up by Tenneco, owner of Case-IH. At first, the lime-green Steiger 1000s continued to roll off the production line, but in 1987, they underwent a transformation and were now finished in Case-IH red and black. Out went the old big cat names, and in came a more sober designation – Lions and Tigers were now the 9000 series. The Puma became the 9110, the Bearcat the 9130 and so on, right through the range.

Some Steiger dealers were so perturbed by this that they made up their own Steiger decals for the new supertractors, but it wasn't until 1995 that Case-IH realised its mistake in ditching such a highly respected name, and brought back the Steiger badge. Still, whatever the badge, Steiger's place in tractor history is clear. It may not have been the pioneer of four-wheel-drive supertractors, but it was certainly the populariser. No-one offered a wider range, and built so many of them.

Versatile

Canadian versatility

The D-145 was the top-power tractor of those Series I Versatiles, with a 7.7-litre Cummins V8.

Versatile was a supertractor pioneer, not that it was the first in the field. In fact, when the D100 appeared in 1966, Steiger had already been in production for half a decade, and Wagner for far longer. Of the mainstream manufacturers, John Deere had offered its four-wheel-drive 8010 back in 1959.

All these were low-production machines that cost a great deal of money however, putting them well out of reach of most farmers.

Versatile's masterstroke was to produce a four-wheel drive supertractor for the price of a conventional machine. The company had built itself up on the strength of offering reliable farm machinery at lower-than-average prices, thanks to simple design and mass production. The D100 simply embodied the same principles applied to a supertractor. It was a huge success, and Versatile Manufacturing of Canada never looked back.

The Versatile story is one of unremitting hard work, of building a big successful business from nothing – the American (or in this case Canadian) dream made real. Peter Pakosh came from Polish stock. His parents met in Pennsylvania, but the Canadian Government's policy of selling immigrants 160 acres of land for $10 induced them to move north in 1908. Emil and Klawda Pakosh built up a successful farm in Saskatchewan, but it became clear that Peter, their eldest son, had an aptitude for engineering. On leaving high school, he thought of becoming a teacher, but that idea was soon dropped, and he moved to Winnipeg in the 1930s to train as an engineer. As a qualified draughtsman, he would still go home to help out on the farm, and in 1940 was delighted to find that his father had finally bought a tractor. That same year, he landed a job with tractor maker Massey Harris.

The young Pakosh was ambitious, and after Massey turned down his application to move into the product design department, he decided to go it alone. He had already designed a simple but effective grain auger, and in 1946 went into limited production, helped by his brother-in-law Roy Robinson, who would be a crucial part of Versatile until the 1970s. Together, they set up the Hydraulic Engineering Company, although 'Versatile' was the brand name almost from the start.

Hydraulic's range grew rapidly, to include a sprayer, a harrow draw bar, and a self-propelled swather. Encouraged by this success, Peter Pakosh left Massey Harris in the spring of 1951, to devote himself to Versatile. The company did well, with sales exceeding $1 million in 1957, then doubling in the next three years. Combine harvesters joined the range, and even a serious factory fire did little to check the company's meteoric progress.

The badge got it right first time: 'Versatiles' proved to be just that, seeing much work beyond the farm.

How it began. The D-100 and cab-fitted D-125 were the first in a long line of Canadian-built Versatiles.

Right: The Cummins engine produced (as the badge suggested) 145hp, enough to keep Versatile customers happy, at least for the time being.

Far right: With the Series I, Versatile proved it was possible to build a four-wheel-drive tractor for little more than the price of a conventional machine.

Below: A Series I Versatile, with a big diesel under the bonnet. Few buyers took the Chrysler or Ford V8 petrol options.

Adding a tractor to the line-up was a logical progression, but there seemed little point in trying to compete with the big manufacturers head on, so Peter Pakosh had other ideas. 'I'd been fascinated by the possibility of producing an inexpensive four-wheel-drive tractor for several years,' he later recalled, 'and we'd kicked around its potential. The trick would be to design one that wouldn't be a luxury. To mass produce such a machine was a radical move.' The conventional wisdom was that there simply wasn't a big enough market for an affordable four-wheel drive tractor, but a report from the University of Manitoba, underlining the efficiency benefits of big 4x4s, convinced Pakosh that this was the way to go.

When it was announced in 1966, the D100 looked very much like a big Steiger or Wagner, but on a smaller scale. Like those giants of the prairies, it had an articulated chassis and four equal-sized wheels. It was less powerful than the big boys, with 100hp at the drawbar and 128hp at the engine. Unusually, this was a British Ford unit, the 6.0-litre six-cylinder 2704E. Customers who really insisted on a petrol engine could opt for the G100, with a 5.2-litre Chrysler V8, mustering slightly more engine hp, the same at

the drawbar. The diesel was far more popular, with 75 per cent of buyers choosing that option. Either way, the transmission was three speeds forward and one reverse, with a four-speed transfer case.

Befitting its Versatile heritage, the D100 had few frills, and you could not order a cab, even as an option, but the payback was a list price of less than $10,000, a real bargain at the time.

The 700 was now Versatile's lead-in tractor, with 230hp from a 9.0-litre Cummins V8.

With the Series II tractors in the mid-1970s, Versatile moved up into Steiger territory.

Below: With the Series II machines, Versatile left its lightweight roots behind and once being established in the supertractor market, the Canadians were able to offer a complete range of machines.

Bottom: A Series II 800 with a 235hp 14.0-litre straight-six; still Cummins, and now Versatile's engine supplier of choice.

Versatile's advertising pulled no punches, and the marketing men calculated that a D100 would save its owner more than $13,000 over a ten-year life, and that was just on the purchase price. With an operating weight of 6.25 tons, the Versatiles were lighter than the heavyweight opposition, so their lower power wasn't the disadvantage it seemed. Little wonder that the first batch of 100 tractors sold out in 1966. Versatile was well and truly in the supertractor business.

Some farmers wanted more power in the same good-value package, so the D100 was rapidly followed up in 1967 with the D118, G125 and

Specification

1966 VERSATILE D100

Engine	Ford 2704E
Engine type	Water-cooled, in-line 6
Aspiration	n/a
Capacity	6.0 litres
Power @ flywheel	128hp
Power @ drawbar	100hp
Transmission	12 x 4
Top speed	16.4mph
Operating weight	14,000lb
Turning radius	13ft
Fuel capacity	54gal

D145. 'Versatile gives you a choice of powerful engines' trumpeted the adverts. The D118 was the new base diesel, using a 5.8-litre Cummins V6 offering, as the name suggested, 118hp at the drawbar, with 135hp at the engine.

There was still a petrol option, but this was now sourced from Ford, an industrial 6.4-litre V8 producing 125hp at the drawbar. This was the least expensive Versatile tractor, at $8,600, and for farmers likely to use their supertractor less intensively, perhaps the most economic option.

The D118 came in at just under $10,000, although for a while the D100 was still listed at the same price. Finally, the range was topped out by the $12,200 D145, whose 7.7-litre Cummins V8 diesel produced 145hp at the drawbar. Still no Steiger in horsepower terms but a new record for Versatile. It might have been the most expensive Versatile tractor yet, but the company's advertising underlined how it would, in the long run, save the farmer money: 'Your most profitable investment for profitable farming.'

Collectively, these tractors were known as the Series I Versatiles, and there were several changes apart from the new power units. A cab joined the list of options, but just as significant was the new heavy-duty transmission. This was built in-house by Versatile, and designed specifically for tractor use. Some supertractors used truck transmissions which could prove unable to cope with the high stresses of field work, vulnerable to overheating, and subsequent failure.

Naturally, there were no such problems with the Versatile transmission. It offered nine forward speeds and three reverse, with working speeds of 3.1, 3.7, 4.2, 4.8, 5.4 and 6.3mph. Another new feature was hydrostatic power steering, which allowed one hand operation. The demand was so high that the company had to

add over 17,000sq ft of floor space to its factory at Fort Garry.

Despite the high demand for its production tractors, Versatile continued to experiment. A prototype skidder tractor for the timber industry was built in the early 1970s, but this never went into production. More fruitful was the hydrostatic drive project. Peter Pakosh had long been fascinated by hydraulic power (as his

Top of the range and the 'Grandaddy of them all', the 300hp 900 of 1975.

Series II Versatiles could pull big implements and work big fields. This is an 850, one of eight models in the series.

Versatile's answer was to combine both systems in the Model 300 Hydro-Mech, launched in 1973. Powered by a 6.2-litre Cummins V6 diesel, this offered hydrostatic drive via a hydraulic pump and motor, with infinite speed control between zero and 7.8mph, forward or reverse. For heavy tillage work, the driver could change to hydro-mechanical mode, which again used the hydrostatic speed control between 1.9mph and 7.8mph. Finally, they could opt for full mechanical mode in low or high range, giving top speeds of 9.7 and 15.4mph respectively.

The 300 was an innovative attempt to give the best of both worlds – the low speed control of hydrostatic, with the heavy duty and high-speed capabilities of mechanical transmission. Versatile decided not to pursue the idea however, and the tractor was dropped after only 200 had been built, although many of these are still in use in Canada and the USA.

'Series 2. Today's Investment for the Future.' The second generation of Versatile supertractors, launched over 1974–76 brought lots of detail improvements. There were several changes to make servicing easier, and there were improved, more comfortable cabs. The transmission across the range was Versatile's own constant-mesh 12-speed, which included five field speeds

For 1977, the 500 was a new 'baby' Versatile of just 192hp (it's all relative).

The 500 lasted only a couple of years, but a more innovative small Versatile was about to be unveiled.

company name demonstrated), and launched a hydrostatic drive swather in 1968, followed by a hydrostatic combine. Hydrostatic drives – using hydraulic motors in each wheel in place of a conventional transmission – have many advantages. They are more simple to operate than mechanical transmissions, have fewer parts, and give more precise speed control, but they are also less efficient, especially in heavy drawbar work.

offering (on the big 900) 4mph to 7.2mph, plus a top road speed of 14.3mph.

Once again, Cummins power predominated. The range kicked off with the 230hp 700, using a 555 V8; the 800 offered 235hp from its 14.0-litre Cummins straight-six, while the 850 had a turbocharged version of the same engine, and 280hp at 2,100rpm. The 1976 range of four tractors was topped by the 900, with a 14.8-litre Cummins V8, and a genuine 300hp at 2,400rpm. This was 'The GRANDADDY of them all … a tractor with total heavy-duty construction which provides dependable performance unequalled by others in the market today. The Model 900 is THE tractor. THE tractor that turns those large field chores into smaller ones.' Not only that, but the 900 was Versatile's biggest, most powerful tractor yet, a move up into Steiger territory.

One of the biggest tractors ever built, but Big Roy was doomed to remain a one-off prototype.

Despite a pivot-steer chassis, the 30ft long Big Roy was not as tight turning as a conventional supertractor.

Top: Big Roy was a massive machine in every sense, but a looming recession put a stop to production before it started.

Above: Eight-wheel drive was deemed the only way to get all that power to the ground efficiently.

Right: Could Big Roy have worked? It certainly had its flaws and seemed to confirm that 500hp was the practical ceiling for supertractors.

Specification

1977 VERSATILE 950

Engine	Cummins VT-903
Engine type	Water-cooled V8
Capacity	14.8 litres
Aspiration	Turbo
Power @ flywheel	348hp @ 2,400rpm
Transmission	12 x 4
Top speed	14.1mph
Av shipping weight	20,850lb
Min turning radius	17ft
Fuel capacity	154gal

And now for something completely different: The Versatile 256 bi-directional tractor, left, would run happily in either direction.

So successful was the 150 bi-directional, that it led to a long line of 'push-pull' tractors, including this 100hp 276 in 1984.

This range of four Series 2s soon became eight, the mid-range bolstered by the six-cylinder 750 and its turbocharged equivalent, the 825. At the top of the range, the 900 was overtaken by the 950, with a turbocharged version of the big Cummins V8, and 348hp. Weighing 9.3 tons ready to work, the 950 would be part of the Versatile range right through to 1982. The work rates of these giant tractors was phenomenal. Even the 850, when fitted with dual wheels, could pull implements up to 60ft wide at

5–6mph, working 45–50 acres an hour.

For a while at least, big was beautiful, and there seemed no limit to the power and size of supertractors. That was the thinking behind Versatile's Big Roy, an eight-wheel prototype that was built in 1976. Everything about Big Roy (named after Roy Robinson, co-founder of the company) was big. The Cummins turbo-intercooled six-cylinder diesel delivered 600hp at 2,100rpm.

Even Versatile's dependable 12-speeder couldn't cope with this much horsepower, so a new six-speed unit was designed specifically for Big Roy. All eight wheels were driven, via four axles, the idea being that having this much rubber was the only way to transfer all that power to the ground without excessive wheel slip. The only problem was that the wheels were in line, so soil compaction was worse than with a conventional dual- or triple-wheel set-up. It measured just over 30ft from front to back, was 11ft high and tipped the scales at 25.7 tons. The fuel tank held 463 gallons of diesel.

The tractor's sheer size brought problems of its own, for the driver sat low behind tinted glass,

with fine visibility to the front, but little to the rear or sides. The rear view was provided via a video screen in the cab, linked to a camera overlooking the hitch. Even with that help, Big Roy wasn't the most nimble of tractors. Its articulation allowed 40° of steering either way (plus 10° of oscillation, in an attempt to keep all eight wheels on the ground over lumps and bumps), but this still added up to a turning radius of 26.6ft – even the big 950 Versatile could manage just under 17ft.

Big Roy was a genuine working prototype, not a showpiece, and it certainly made an impact when unveiled to the US farming press, with impressive field trials as well as its paper specification. But although there were some serious enquiries, the hard fact was that American farming was facing a downturn, and Versatile hesitated before going into production. It already had a healthy 30 per cent of the supertractor market in North America, and Big Roy would have made an imposing flagship. It could also have turned into an expensive white elephant, with unsold tractors gathering dust on dealer lots as the farming recession bit. It would also have

needed a complete set of special implements to match its size and by 1980, all ideas of producing Versatile's biggest ever tractor had been abandoned. The one and only prototype remains on display at the Manitoba Agricultural Museum in Austin, Manitoba, Canada.

At the other end of the scale, the new 500 was unveiled in 1977, which had an 8.3-litre six-cylinder Cummins of 'just' 192hp. It had its own

Now owned by Cornat Industries, Versatile updated its supertractors for 1978 as the Labour Force range.

Spacious cabs with fine visibility had long been standard on Versatiles.

All Labour Force Versatiles had 42° of articulation and 30° of oscillation.

The mid-range 875 offered 280hp, and the whole line used Cummins Constant Power diesels.

transmission – a 15-speed unit compared with the 12-speed of the rest of the range, allowing a road speed of up to 17.4mph. With a live PTO (something the short-lived 300 had offered) and adjustable wheel treads, the 500 was designed for corn and soya bean row-crops.

That 500 actually only lasted a couple of years, but another new tractor launched by Versatile at

the time had a far more lasting influence. The 150 hardly qualifies as a supertractor, but it is worth mentioning here because it was so central to the Versatile story. The 150 was a bi-directional or 'push-pull' tractor, the world's first, with a reversible driving position that allowed it to be worked equally well in either direction, with implements at either end. With the successful return of hydrostatic drive, the 150 was easy to operate as well, and was a hit with farmers – there was nothing quite like it in 1977. So successful was Versatile's bi-directional tractor

Specification

1977 VERSATILE 1080 'BIG ROY'

Engine	Cummins KTA-1150
Engine type	Water-cooled in-line 6
Aspiration	Turbo-aftercooled
Capacity	18.9 litres
Power @ engine	600hp @ 2,100rpm
Transmission	6-speed manual
Top speed	13.2mph
Operating weight	57,568lb
Turning radius	26.6ft
Fuel capacity	457gal

that it spawned a whole dynasty of 'push-pulls', the 85hp 256 and 100hp 276 in 1984, the New Holland 9030 in 1990, and the TV140 in 1998.

Meanwhile, Peter Pakosh and Big Roy Robinson were thinking of retirement. Talks with farm machinery maker Hesston came to nothing, but in 1977 Versatile was sold to Cornat Industries, another Canadian concern. The following year, the supertractor line-up was updated as the Labour Force range. There were new Cummins Constant Power diesels, so called because they offered maximum power up to 400rpm below the rated engine speed, making this less susceptible to bogging down in tough sections of soil. The Labour Force had more drawbar pull than the old tractors, and better traction. They were more manoeuvrable too, with 42° of articulation in either direction, and a new centre pivot chassis which allowed 30° of oscillation.

As launched, there were four tractors in the range, which replaced the earlier Series 2s. All were turbocharged, and the base 835 offered 230hp from its 14.0-litre six. The 855 had an uprated version of the same engine, as did the 875, with 280hp at 2,100rpm. Topping the range was the latest incarnation of the 900, the 935, with 330hp from its 14.8-litre Cummins V8. The

range was filled out in 1980 by the 895, which filled the gap between the 875 and the 935, using a 310hp aftercooled version of the familiar 14.0-litre straight-six. Meanwhile, the row-crop 500 was replaced by the 555. Nicknamed the 'Triple Nickel' in the USA, this fulfilled the same brief as its predecessor, that of a row-crop tractor for medium and large farms. Power was boosted to

The Versatile 895 of 310hp, which slotted in below the 330hp 935 flagship machine.

The 500 had an update as well, as the 555 Triple Nickel, now with 210hp.

Specification

1982 VERSATILE 1150

Engine	Cummins KTA 1150
Engine type	Water-cooled in-line 6
Capacity	18.9 litres
Aspiration	Turbo-intercooled
Power @ flywheel	470hp @ 2,100rpm
Power @ drawbar	400hp
Transmission	8 x 4 manual
Top speed	16.0mph
Av shipping weight	46,500lb
Min turning radius	15.2ft
Fuel capacity	330gal

210hp from a Cummins turbo V8, while the standard transmission was still 15-speed, constant-mesh. The 555 proved to be highly adaptable, able to carry out cultivating and planting work for which the really large tractors were too big.

Many of those 'Triple Nickels' were exported to Australia, and by this time, Versatile was a world player in the supertractor market. That was underlined when a deal was signed with Fiat, which sold Versatiles in Europe, painted and badged as its own, from the 230hp Fiat 44-23 to the 350hp 44-55.

Big Roy might never have made it to production, but Versatile did eventually find a use for that massive Cummins six-cylinder engine. The 18.9-litre unit powered the new 1150 tractor of 1982, now offering 470hp in turbo-intercooled form, and it wasn't just a blown-up version of the smaller tractors. The 1150 was designed with comprehensive system of electronics and microprocessors, monitoring everything from exhaust temperature to transmission oil pressure. The transmission was of course, Versatile's own, an eight-speed constant-

Above: A perfect view of a classic four-wheel-drive pivot-steer supertractor.

Opposite: Many Triple Nickels were exported to Australia, while North American farmers tended to favour the more powerful Versatiles.

Below: One of the Series III Versatiles launched in 1983, with more black paint and new Cummins diesels.

Top: Takeover by Ford New Holland brought another new colour scheme to Versatile tractors; the Designation 6 models continued in production with the new owner.

Above: The 946 was Versatile's mid-range tractor of the time, and had a 12-speed powershift option.

mesh unit with four reverse speeds, and the option of a 12-speed powershift.

Meanwhile, the smaller, or rather, not so large, Versatiles were updated through the 1980s. As the 1983 Series IIIs, they had the latest Cummins Big Cam III power units with improved fuel efficiency, plus a new cab with multi-adjustable seat and steering wheel. The 945, 955 and 975 replaced the 855, 935 and 950 respectively, and had up to 360hp.

Two years later, they became the Designation 6 Series. Instantly recognisable with a new bold grille, and finished in Versatile's traditional red, yellow and black colours, they came with better visibility and more comfort. The engines were new too, although Versatile remained loyal to its long-time supplier, and the latest 10.0-litre Cummins six was claimed to be 10 per cent more fuel efficient than the 14.0-litre unit it replaced. The higher powered tractors carried on with the

bigger engine though, with 360hp for the 976.

The options now included row-crop adjustable axles, a 1,000rpm PTO and high-clearance, 42in tyres as well as mechanical or powershift transmissions. The range was extended downwards in 1986 with the 756, a 190hp tractor which was built to order, to keep the price down. At the same time, the big 1150 was updated to Designation 6 specification, as the 1156, with Whisper Quiet cab and an electronic instrument display.

But things weren't going well for Versatile. The 1980s were hard times in the farm machinery business across the world, especially so in North America, where Versatile was hit hard. Peter Pakosh later recalled: 'The economy started to slip. Grain prices started to go down. Cornat Industries started to get themselves in trouble at Versatile. They started to realize that maybe they had taken a bigger bite than they could chew …

A new century, a new owner, and the Buhler Versatiles carried on working.

A two-wheel-drive International gives scale to this 555, the 'small' Versatile.

Best known for its giant supertractors such as this 895, Versatile started out with a smaller, 100hp machine.

Cornat stripped Versatile of quite a bit of assets, as they were having problems with their operation in Vancouver.'

Cornat wanted to sell, and John Deere showed interest in taking over the tractor business, but this was barred by the Justice Department, as the result would have commanded over half the sales of four-wheel-drive machines in North America. Versatile's Winnipeg factory actually ceased production for much of 1986, but in early 1987 it was announced that Ford New Holland had bought the company. It was late July before the factory reopened and big Versatile tractors began rolling out the doors once again.

At first, the previous line-up was continued, the 846, 876, 946, 976 and 1156, and they even retained the Versatile colour scheme. Under the new ownership, this could not last, and for 1989,

the range, still with no major changes, came in Ford's corporate blue colour scheme. The Versatile badge was still there, but smaller than that of Ford. One advance was the option of a 12-speed powershift across the range, and load-sensor hydraulics which delivered pressure only when needed.

Within a few years however, Ford was having doubts of its own. It wanted to get out of tractors altogether, and in 1991 sold its New Holland stake to Fiat, which of course included Versatile. As part of the deal, the Ford badge was still worn up to the year 2000, although Fiat was sufficiently savvy to realise that the respected Versatile badge had to stay as well. Still with Ford badges, the Designation 6 Versatiles were replaced by the 80 Series in 1994: 9280 (250hp), 9480 (300hp), 9680 (350hp) and 9880 (400hp). Some

things didn't change though, and the entire range was still Cummins powered. These were soon updated as the 82 Series, with more power all round (to 425hp, in the case of the 9882), more hydraulic flow, easier servicing, and a more comfortable cab.

So, Versatile had finally appeared to have attained corporate stability, as the supertractor specialist within a global company. Except that it didn't work out quite like that as in 2000, New Holland merged with Case to form CNH Global. The resulting corporation was so huge that the authorities insisted that some sections be sold off first, to prevent a monopoly situation. This meant Versatile, but fortunately a local buyer was on hand, Buhler Industries of Winnipeg – which bought the name and the factory, and production carried on. In fact, to emphasise the end of the

New Holland era, the tractors were relaunched in January 2001, in Versatile red and yellow, although this was soon changed to Buhler's red and black.

By 2006, the Buhler Versatile four-wheel drives covered a similar power range to Versatiles of the previous decade. Collectively known as the 2000 Series, they spanned five models, from the 290hp 2290 to the 425hp 2425. All were Cummins powered, by 10.8-litre or 14.0-litre turbo-intercooled sixes. The transmission was a mechanical QuadShift, with 12-speed powershift still an option across the range, as was a PTO and three-point hitch.

And so Versatile rolled on into the 21st century, 40 years after that first supertractor was unveiled, and is still acknowledged as one of the world leaders in giant, four-wheel-drive tractors.

The twin wheels on this Versatile 850 maximise traction and minimise wheel slippage.

Wagner

Pioneer from Portland

One of the earliest Wagner farm tractors, this TRS-9 was built in 1956. Surely it deserves a better fate than this?

Ask most tractor enthusiasts who pioneered the pivot-steer four-wheel-drive supertractor, and you usually get one of two answers: Steiger or Versatile. It's an understandable mistake, as those two were immensely successful across the world, not just in North America, and survived in name right into the 1990s. However, Wagner Tractor Inc of Portland, Oregon pre-dated both those well-known names by many years, and was the true originator of the pivot-steer supertractor.

There were seven Wagner brothers – Eddie, Bill, Gus, Walter, Harold, Irvin and Elmer – and back in 1922, they set up in business as Mixermobile, having designed and built a mobile machine that could mix and distribute concrete on construction sites. Over the years, the prolific Wagners would design many other items of construction machinery, with names such as Scoopmobile, Dozermobile and others, which suggested their use. Some of these had four-wheel drive, and many where very successful.

Elmer Wagner was said to have got the idea for applying this experience to farm tractors from a machine he spotted when coming home from

Europe during the Second World War. After the war, the brothers began experimenting with pivot-steering, and the Dozermobile of 1950 used this system. At first, experiments had centred on pivot-steering alone, but the brothers soon found that on uneven ground, the machine could have one or two wheels in the air, unable to transmit power. The answer was axle oscillation, allowing both axles to follow the contours independently, thus keeping all four wheels in contact with the terra firma, and thus transmitting power, all the time.

The key to all this was the Wagner's patented Pow-R-Flex coupling, which used a hydrostatic steering system of two pins and a single hydraulic cylinder with two drive-shaft joints delivering the power to the rear axle. This obviously had an application in farming for rough terrain, which was a departure for the Wagners, as they had previously concentrated on construction, mining and forestry machinery. A prototype pivot-steer was built up, based on a Ford Ferguson tractor,

It may not look that prepossessing, but this is a pioneer of the supertractor concept, courtesy of the Wagner brothers.

The early Wagners proved popular with farmers in difficult terrain, being faster and cheaper than a crawler.

Above: Move into the early 1960s, and Wagner is under new ownership, with this WA-14 typical of the range.

Right: After experiencing unreliability with Buda and Waukesha engines, Wagner switched to Cummins power.

Far right: The key to it all: twin multi-joint driveshafts allowed the pivot-steer Wagner to have oscillating axles, a key advantage for any supertractor.

and it worked well enough on Gus Wagner's farm to encourage the brothers to push ahead with the project. It has to be said that all of them were inveterate engineers, continually developing and improving the machines they made. It has been said that no two Wagner tractors that left the factory were ever the same.

The first pivot-steer Wagner tractors were sold in 1951, but it was another three years before an agricultural version was finally announced. At 64hp, the first Wagner TR-6 was hardly a high-horsepower machine, using a Waukesha 190LB six-cylinder engine, although it was soon joined by the 85hp TR-9 and 160hp TR-14, both Buda powered. However, ultimate power was not a big issue, as the Wagner's unique combination of four-wheel drive, pivot-steering and oscillating axles made them more effective than many rivals in difficult farming country.

This was especially true of crawlers from International and Caterpillar, which were the farmers' favourites in hilly country. These crawlers were reliable and could get through anything, but they were also slow, expensive and maintenance-intensive. The wheeled Wagner did not have the ultimate mud-plugging ability of a good crawler, but it was much faster and more efficient on harder ground. An independent test in 1955, comparing a TR-14 with a crawler, showed the Wagner to work nearly twice as fast, ploughing 80 acres in the time it took the crawler to cover 50. It also used slightly less fuel in the process and so running a Wagner in place of a crawler could save between 20 and 50 per cent on running costs.

Above left: Wagners were no-frills machines, tools to do a job.

Above: The lube schedule for a hard-working machine engine, torque converter and power steering; oil to be checked daily, and grease points attended to.

Below: No three-point hitch on this WA-14, but Wagner tractors weren't intended for general field work.

Specification

1956 WAGNER TR-9

Engine	Cummins
Engine type	Water-cooled in-line 4
Capacity	8.1 litres
Power @ engine	125hp @ 1,800rpm
Power @ PTO	87hp
Transmission	10 x 2 manual
Top speed	15mph
Operating weight	15,445lb
Min turning radius	13.25ft
Fuel capacity	60gal

Just in case the operator missed it the first time, this provides the oil specifications and servicing needs for every major component.

Wagners weren't cheap, but many farmers realised the huge savings to be made with this sort of work rate, and the brothers found themselves a thriving new market sector. After just two and a half years, they had sold over 350 tractors to farmers, worth over $6 million. Forty-three dealers across the USA and western Canada were promoting this new concept in farm machinery. Suitably encouraged, the Wagners launched their most powerful farm tractor yet, the 300hp Cummins-powered TR24.

Those early tractors were not without their troubles. The Buda and Waukesha engines proved so unreliable that many early Wagners were returned to the factory to receive Cummins replacements, and the TR-9 tested at the University of Nebraska in 1957 was also Cummins powered. It was a good choice, as Cummins was a widely respected supplier of good, reliable diesel engines. Truck axles used on some early tractors failed too, although this was cured by switching to Clark industrial paired axles. The Clark components also included planetary drives with a 3:1 reduction, which cut the amount of torque sent through the driveline, reducing stress and the number of failures.

By 1961, Wagner's farm tractor business was very well established, attractive enough to be snapped up by the FWD Corporation. It was a time of expansion, with production moved to a larger factory in Portland and a new range of tractors launched. The Wagner WA range (the letters standing for Wagner Agricultural) was wider than ever, but the WA-6, WA-9, WA-14 and WA-24 were all similar to the TR series that preceded them.

One entirely new model was the WA-4, powered by a three-cylinder 3-71 Detroit Diesel

Wagner's swansong was to build WA-14s and WA-17s (this is a '17) for John Deere. The agreement led to the end of Wagner production.

engine of 98hp. It also had a three-point hitch, underlining Wagner's determination to appeal to a wider cross-section of farmers. The following year, the 3-71 was replaced by the four-cylinder 4-53 Detroit, rated as 120hp at 2,500rpm. Meanwhile, the WA-9 now used a six-cylinder Cummins C160, and the range was topped by the 220hp WA-14, 250hp WA-17 and 300hp WA-24.

Behind the optimism, Wagner tractors were, unfortunately, entering a period of instability. FWD decided to concentrate on its fire trucks and axles, and sold the Wagner side of the business to Raygo, whose tenure proved even shorter, and the company produced just two WA-24s. By 1968, the future of Wagner tractors did not look promising. Unlike the new line-ups from Steiger and Versatile, they had not been kept up to date, and it was nearly 15 years since those first TR-6s had amazed American farmers.

However, there did appear to be a lifeline, in the form of John Deere, which wanted an established pivot-steer supertractor to enhance its range. Deere of course, had launched its own supertractor back in 1959, but the 8010 proved troublesome and short-lived. The deal with Wagner promised a contract for 100 WA-14s and

Specification

1969 WAGNER WA-17 (JOHN DEERE)

Engine	Cummins NT855C1
Engine type	Water-cooled in-line 6
Aspiration	Turbo
Power @ flywheel	280hp @ 2,100rpm
Transmission	10 x 2 manual
Top speed	15mph
Av shipping weight	28,280lb
Fuel capacity	100gal

17s supplied in the John Deere livery. In the event, only 51 tractors had been delivered before John Deere's own 7020 pivot-steer vehicle was ready. This spelt the end of the contract, which included a clause forbidding Wagner from building a rival tractor, meant the end of Wagner production as well.

It was a sad end, but the fact remains that the Wagner brothers really did pioneer the four-wheel-drive supertractor concept, showing the potential of this layout for farming. Without their work, would Steiger, Versatile, Big Bud and the rest have followed with such tractors?

Not a Wagner, but a Schafer, which was built in Kansas from 1961, and arguably influenced by the Wagner brothers' pioneering work.

White
Low-profile

In its own way, the White Field Boss was quite innovative, a low-slung supertractor designed to appeal to row-crop farmers.

The short and rather tangled history of White supertractors highlights the difficult times the US tractor industry was going through in the 1970s and '80s. Their eventual fate was determined not by any technical consideration, or how well they worked in the field, but by a depressed market and the weakness of the companies which made them.

White itself had no agricultural background. The White Motor Corporation built trucks, but decided to diversify into tractors, buying up the Oliver concern in 1960. Cockshutt Farm Equipment – the Canadian company that built both tractors and combines – followed in 1962, as well as Minneapolis-Moline in 1963. White therefore found itself managing three separate tractor lines, each with its distinctive heritage and brand loyalty, and it was not until 1969 that all three were consolidated under a common umbrella, White Farm Equipment.

Production of the first tractor to wear the White badge began later that same year, although the White Plainsman was no more or less than a rebadged, repainted Minneapolis-Moline A4T 1400 or 1600. As such, it used MM running gear including a choice of 139hp, 154hp or 169hp, diesel or LPG engines. Exactly the same trick was performed with the Oliver 2455/2655, finished in Oliver green/white, but really exactly the same A4T underneath.

At first, the Plainsman was sold only in Canada, but there can be little doubt that White's long-term aim was to drop the old names and bring all corporate tractor production together under the White brand name. The Plainsman was only offered during 1970, but in January '72 White announced that a new range of tractors was on the drawing board – they were called Field Boss, and they would be marketed only as Whites.

Specifications

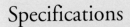

1974 WHITE 4-150 FIELD BOSS

Engine	Caterpillar 3208
Engine type	Water-cooled V8
Capacity	10.4 litres
Power @ flywheel	175hp @ 2,800rpm
Power @ PTO	150hp
Transmission	18 x 6, partial powershift
Top speed	19.2mph
Av shipping weight	20,000lb
Min turning radius	15.1ft
Fuel capacity	143gal

1983 WFE 4-270 FIELD BOSS

Engine	Caterpillar
Engine type	Water-cooled in-line 6
Aspiration	Turbo
Capacity	10.5 litres
Power @ flywheel	270hp @ 2,100rpm
Power @ PTO	239hp
Transmission	16 x 4, partial powershift
Top speed	19.9mph
Av shipping weight	29,060lb
Min turning radius	19.5ft
Fuel capacity	196gal

This was bad news for loyalists to the old marques of Cockshutt, Oliver and Minneapolis-Moline, but when they were unveiled in 1974, the new White Field Boss range looked modern and up to the minute. The new silver and charcoal grey colour scheme was pretty classy, and the Field Boss had a modern, squared-off look that was quite distinctive.

Not only that, but it lived up to White's description of a 'low-profile' tractor, nestling

Top: It looked modern and distinctive, but the Field Boss made use of existing parts.

Above: As this view of a 4-150 shows, the White was a more compact tractor than any Steiger or Versatile.

Top: Caterpillar provided the 3208 V8 diesel, rated at either 150hp or 180hp, depending on model.

Above: The Field Boss 4-180 later became the 4-210, thanks to a different means of measuring horsepower.

Right: Ultimately, White's attempt to launch a new tractor line ended in failure with the company losing millions of dollars a year.

down between its eight big wheels in a way that no other supertractor did. White management had decided to build a smaller, more manageable type of supertractor, aimed specifically at row-crop farmers rather than the wheat barons. So the Field Boss used two Oliver two-wheel drive final drive housings, one forwards, one backwards, which made the whole tractor relatively narrow as well as low profile.

White Farm Equipment brought all its research and development onto one site at Libertyville, Illinois, in 1975, all the better to bring on the expanding line-up of White Field Bosses, which included a range of two-wheel drive machines. Despite its investment in R&D, it wasn't worth the company building its

A dilapidated Field Boss 4-210 and a 4-150. A 270hp range-topper followed later.

Under new ownership, the two- and four-wheel-drive Whites were rebranded WFE, but this phase did not last long.

own engine for what was essentially a niche tractor, so it bought a 10.4-litre V8 diesel in from Caterpillar, which delivered 150hp at the PTO, hence the name. This came at a time when supertractor makers were beginning to quote engine or flywheel horsepower figures, instead of those at the PTO or drawbar. It was a confusing time, not least when White upgraded the 4-150 into the 4-175 in 1979 – this wasn't the power boost it seemed, simply

that it took its name from engine, rather than the PTO horsepower!

The 4-150 was soon followed by a 4-180, based on the same running gear; even the engine was the same 3208 Caterpillar unit, with the fuelling turned up to produce more power. It had a 12-speed transmission, while the 4-150 employed an 18-speed in the form of six speeds in three-ranges with an Over/Under Powershift. To ease the strain on those Oliver axles, the 180 also added planetary drives to reduce the torque loading. Choose a 4-180, and you also had the option of a heater and air conditioning. Just as those requoted power figures had given the 4-150 an apparent boost, so the 4-180 later became the 4-210.

The Field Bosses were a brave attempt to launch a new tractor line and a new brand, using the best of what was available, but they could not prevent White's further financial slide. It had lost $69 million in 1975 alone, and in 1980 after facing Chapter 11 bankruptcy, the company sold off its White Farm Equipment arm to the TIC Investment Corporation. Tractor production was resumed, taking on a new look in 1982, when the White name was dropped in favour of a WFE logo, and the silver/grey colour scheme replaced by white with a bright red stripe.

The following year, the 4-175 and 4-210 were replaced by two powered-up models, retaining

Caterpillar power, although now from different engines. The new WFE 4/225 was really a carry-over of the old Field Boss, but now with a turbocharger added to the Caterpillar V8, to give 225 engine hp at 2,600rpm, and 195hp at the PTO. The 18-speed Over/Under Powershift still featured.

The 4/270 on the other hand, although similar in appearance, was substantially new, and really the only new tractor to join the range since the original. It had a new, larger frame, with a new powershift transmission that the company said had been under development for a decade. With partial powershift over four ranges, this gave 16 forward speeds in total. The engine was new too,

a 10.5-litre Caterpillar six, very slightly larger than the V8, and offering 270hp at 2,100rpm, with 239hp at the PTO.

TIC struggled on with the WFE Field Boss tractors, although it had its doubts about their viability. This was confirmed when it sold the line to Allied Products in 1985. Allied already owned implement maker New Idea, and set up White-New Idea with ambitions of offering a complete farm equipment range. However, the four-wheel drive Field Bosses were soon dropped. The White name lived on for awhile, even after White-New Idea was taken over by AGCO in 1993, but its distinctive low-profile supertractors were no more.

The White name later resurfaced as part of AGCO, and it is still there today.

Index